MONEY Scraps

MONEY *Scraps*

MATTHEW POPE

"Your story is our priority"

LitPrime Solutions
21250 Hawthorne Blvd
Suite 500, Torrance, CA 90503
www.litprime.com
Phone: 1-800-981-9893

Published by LitPrime Solutions   07/25/2023

ISBN: 979-8-88703-029-6(sc)
ISBN: 979-8-88703-030-2(e)

Library of Congress Control Number: 2022912756

CANADIAN WILDLIFE
FEDERATION

350 Michael Cowpland Drive
Kanata, ON K2M 2W1
T 1 800 563 9453
E info@cwf-fcf.org
CanadianWildlifeFederation.ca

Matthew Pope
2 B732 5555 Periwinkle Lane
Sechelt BC V0N 3A0

Dear friend of Canadian wildlife,

I recently sent you an exclusive 2016 Canadian Wildlife Federation calendar. This was sent to loyal supporters like you to thank them for making our programs and conservation work possible.

While this beautiful calendar was sent as a token of our appreciation, meant to honour your commitment to the Canadian Wildlife Federation, I hope you will be inspired to continue support CWF's work to conserve wildlife and the wild spaces they call home.

Many supporters who have received their 2016 calendar have already renewed their commitment to wildlife. Their gifts will fund vital work to conserve many species of wildlife in the coming year.

If you have already renewed your commitment with a gift, thank you! Please disregard this letter. But if you have not yet sent a donation, please do so today, while you have my letter in your hand.

Your gift will help CWD conserve Canada's amazing wildlife. Any donations would be very much appreciated.

Sincerely,

Wade Luzny CEO, Executive Vice-President

P.S. The Canadian Wildlife Federation relies on the generosity of supporters like you. Together, we can make a positive difference, now and for generations to come. Thank you for your continued support!

P.P.S. Donations postmarked by December 31, 2015 will receive a 2015 tax receipt.

HOW TO HELP WILDLIFE THIS WINTER

During winter, there are many things you can do in your backyard that will a difference for wildlife.

1. **Helping beneficial insects over winter**

   Most beneficial insects stay in Canada over the winter. Providing sheltered spots for them in your garden throughout the season and into spring is the easiest way to help these species flourish. And when the spring comes next year, these beneficial insects eat potential pests, and pollinate your garden.

   You can make space for them by providing habitat spaces, such as:
   - Leaf litter or mulches
   - Tree hollows or under bark – old or dead trees provide great shelter for insects
   - Fallen logs and/or rock piles
   - Dead flower stalks - insects that overwinter as pupae in a protective cocoon (such as butterflies) attach the pupae to their primary source of food
   - Dense vegetation like long grass makes great homes for insects
   - Soil or wood to burrow in – avoid tilling the soil in the fall By providing these habitats, you'll be helping many insects that are vital to our ecosystem.

2. **Building a bat house to provide shelter for bats**

   The Little Brown Bat is in serious trouble. A fungus called white-nose syndrome (WNS) is wiping out entire colonies and is spreading fast. We need to act quickly to save the remainder populations of the Little Brown Bat, and also do what we can to Canada's other species.

Here's how you can help bats today:
- Help increase awareness by building your very own bat house this winter and placing it on your property in the spring.
- Join our advocacy efforts. You can protect bats by helping CWF ensure that they are offered legal protection under the *Species at Risk Act*.
- To learn more about building bat houses, and to stay informed about CWF's advocacy efforts, visit **HelptheBats.ca.**

3. **Provide habitat and food for birds**

Habitat loss and pollution continue to threaten migratory birds like the Whooping Crane, Chimney Swift, and many other species. Other birds are now living closer to human populations, increasing threats from predators such as feral cats, crows, raccoons and other mammals. You can make a difference for Canada's birds.

Here's what you can do right now in your backyard to help birds:
- Build a winter bird roost that will provide songbirds with shelter during the cold months.
- Ensure that your bird feeders are full all winter, and install a cone-shaped predator guard to prevent predators from reaching the feeder and birds.
- Leave a brush pile in the corner of your yard to help create extra shelter for birds, as they can use these piles to escape the worst of the winter cold.

TSA ON THE COAST

GIVING HOPE TODAY

The Salvation Army
Sunshine Coast Ministries
5-682 Gibsons Way
Mailing Address: PO Box 1625
Gibsons, BC V0N 1V0
Telephone: 604-886-3680
Fax: 604-886-3683

December 2015

Dear Friend,

RE: Your Generous Donation:

Thank you for your donation to The Salvation Army-Sunshine Coast Community Ministries. Enclosed with this letter your official **2015 Tax Receipt for Income Tax purposes.**

Your gift will continue to help our local communities on the Sunshine Coast. Some of the programs offered at The Salvation Army include a Monthly Food Bank, a Family & Community Ministries where we distribute emergency food, clothes, furniture, and give various help depending on the need.

There is a hot meal served twice a week and a Daily Bread & Produce Program. We also send children & adults to camp at Camp Sunrise. **Thanks to our supporters in 2015 we are able to provide 1,800 adults and children hampers of food on the Sunshine Coast. Thanks to our bread and produce volunteers and donors in 2015 we will have had over 10,000 visits. Thanks to our lunch and friends volunteers and donors in 2015 we will have served over 4500 hot meals to adults and families on the Sunshine Coast.**

Every gift ensures that everyone has the opportunity to receive healthy meals and programs. Please also note that all money donated to us from the public stays on the Coast to support the ministry here.
Thank you for helping us to help others.

Merry Christmas and May God bless!

Corps Officers/Pastors
Sunshine Coast Ministries

WILLIAM & CATHERINE BOOTH	LINDA BOND	SUSAN MCMILLAN	LARRY MARTIN
FOUNDERS	GENERAL	TERRITORIAL COMMANDER	DIVISONAL COMMANDER

Sept 22 '16

Tony Robins
Coach in a day
(what it is like)

```
                    S
                    T                    A
    P               R                    C
    L               A                    T
    A               T                    I
    N               E                    O
                    G                    N
                    Y
```

Solution

Rmtnow.com

Tony Robbins

The five basic moves of change

1. Emotional state
   How you Feel Affects What Happens to you

2. Focus
   Am I see the opportunities or only the obstacles. Focus on where you want to go

3. Meaning

4. Relationships
   We're all connected to other people love

5. Strategy
   Solve the problems with small action

Facebook

1. Find content
    Ask question

2. Engagement talk about them not you

3. Reach more people
    Boost Button

Big Reason #1

The Source (Mind)
Elements of change

1. Awareness

2. Understanding
    - Meaning different for each person
    - Nothing is anything unless you make it
    - Reality is personal
    - What you mean is what you get
    - Know thyself

To Survive
To keep you alive
    - Mind is based in problems and fears

The Ultimate Life Makeover Video
Personal Environment

Step 1

What do you really want
Keyword

You
Today what do you want (specific)

Step 2
Why do you want this?

Be independent
Poor judgement
Relief and Joy

Anxiety based in fear
Having you believe it is your life
Your mind is your protection director
Don't believe a thought you think
Conscious from the choice in the moment
–Change thought
The 4 Magic words
Say thank you for sharing then insert better thought
Empowering

Step 3
Why not
Why don't you already have it?

Give away too much

Step 4
Strategy/Plan

How

Refrain from letting others take so much away

Three Laws of Thought

1. Ability to control thoughts

2. Ability to remove thought

3. To install thought in phamiled

Power

Step 5
First Action
Think Less
Do more

Refuse some things

Step 6
Commitment
Devour oneself
Unreservedly

I Matt Pope commit to refuse something no matter what Refers this (unreadable)

Jim
$495.00
To change you have to change
Don't wish for less problems more skills
- Steady progress to get there

Wisdom and Faith put with a deposit of activity Anything easy to do is easy not to do

Self service leads success
Self investment leads to fortune
Activity finishes the miracle

Don't finish your education
Self education

Step 7
Reward
Positive Reinforcement
Reward the behavior
Play mugs with coffee or wine

Step 8
The Accelerator
Accountability
To explain what you have done to others

- Your income is your philosophy
- Success is what you attract
- Goal setting philosophy is your guidance

In due time you qualify
You get what you deserve

Communication

- Study and fascinated

8) Abundance
Add mere value
Do more for others
Serving a large number of people or deep

Management of Time

10) Action

Learning leading to Action

Why?
Why not?
Why not you?
Why not now?

1) Philosophy

3) Goals
4) Leadership
5) Lifestyle
6) Communication
7) Influence
8) Abundance
9) Productivity
10) Action

Michelle Audrey
BJ8921S Pescosolido
#1 Strategy
Value

Blogging + FB Ads conversion Ad
Run 3 days for traffic $100 bucks
Facebook live weekly same day & time
Notify
—repeat 25-50 dollars

#1 Fatal mistake
System and Processes
Know your numbers
Install pixels   —content specialized-
Create a daily routine   2017 year of content
Install pixel on website
SEO xx doing monthly
Blogging

SEO
Intent and Content
Refining content needs to match intent
What does it solve?
Different context

Adsplit testing
Website conversion Ad
—Mobile AppInstall
—collect leads for business
    Xx x xx trust
—Target audience
—Delivery optimization
—Placements
    Split testing xx works

–Divides xx into xx
Non-overlapping group xxx
Shown sets with identical creative

Randomization test to conduct fairly not to skew results of group comparison given equal chance in auction distinct difference called variable $1000 for testing ads performance according to campaign objective; then recorded and compared best performing ad xx when testing complete notification and email containing results insights to fuel your next strategy

Choose clicks to website either send traffic to a URL or inside at Facebook
–choose messenger placement
–ad will call to action to send message
–messenger will open up after clicked ad
Build relationships
What we do, how we can help them a bit about yourself.
Custom Audiences
–Video engagement (done)
–Fan page engagement (done)
–Head Forms??

Opened but didn't opt In and opted In

Custom Audiences
Page
–liked
–commented
–shared
Appears for audience and google quality user experience.
Matching product to results.
–updating contents (done to some degree).
–xxx /updated content (done to some degree).

The Power Players Club is perfect for you if your struggling to figure out this "marketing thing"

2. You're a beginner
3. You're a more "seasoned" marketer
4. You're winging it.
5. You're hoping & praying.
6. You want to get coaching and mentorship.
   http:onlinewealthpartner.com/powerplayersclub.
   1. Live "Power Player club sessions"
   Training sessions are recorded ever Wednesday
   2. Both provide step by step

Sessions include

1. Facebook marketing (general & specific)
2. Facebook advertising
3. Content Marketing/Blogging
4. Video Marketing (Done)
5. Copy Writing/Email Marketing (Done)
6. Sales/Recruiting
7. SEO/Search Engine Optimization (Done)
8. Personal Brand Building (Done)
9. Details on the tools we use & how to use them (Done)

   Xan volunteer to be put in the hot seat. (Done)
   Will analyze and critique your ads xx
   –xx things out ahead xx

–Facebook ads
–Landing Page
–Facebook Fan Page
–Blog & Content
–Email Marketing/Copy Writing (Done)

Your gold status as an affiliate
–advanced notification on launches
–insider tips
–rewarded a higher commission

50% US to 30%
–Free ticket to all live events
–Free mastermind at any other support xxwealthpartners

What one skill = an awesome like
Adaptability = key
Connection beyond yourself
When to adapt
Rest and relaxation
Mindfulness

Book
The Dolphin Way (xx.04) Amazon
Dr. Shimi Kang
Play back into life

Harv T. Ecker
Secrets of the Millionaire Mind
Programming+thoughts+feelings+actions = results

Don't have to prove yourself from anger, fear, etc won't be happy.

—think big

Solve problems is an Entrepreneur commitment to creating wealth
—love paying bills
—get in the corridor learn (done).
—admire successful people
—you are 'worthy'
—be a receiver, (nurture yourself).
—start your own business, contract, network, marketing

No ceiling on making money
—have family, friends and money to xx happiness.

Rich Dad, Poor Dad

—Have money work for you
—Buy assets
—Solve problems
—difference between liabilities and assets create income generating assets.
—Don't get mutual funds take risk
—Watch founder of McDonald's move
—Build asset column royalties xx xx assets for example.
—The rich with corporations

People who work for corporations

1. Earn	1. Earn
2. Spend	2. Pay taxes
3. Pay taxes	3. Spend

—Own your own corporation

T. Harv Eker

Jan 22 2017

Secrets of the Millionaire Mind

—scale back

—build your net worth

—financial freedom bank account

—put money in different accounts to invest and create passive income

—substitute investment work energy with other forms of energy.

—comfort cone = wealth zone

—do things inspite of worry, fear, etc.

—order of success rich people. Be, do, have

    Poor people have, do, Be

Rich Dad, Poor Dad

1. Financial literacy
2. Investment strategies
3. The Market
4. The Law

Main Skills of Success

–management of cash flow
–management of systems (including yourself and time with family)
–management of people
–specialized skills are sales and understanding of marketing

Overcoming Obstacles

1. Fear
2. Cynicism
3. Laziness
4. Bad Habits
5. Arrogance

I need a reason greater than reality the power of spirit. Choose daily.

Rich Dad Poor Dad

Warning: Don't listen to poor frightened people
−4. Master a formula then learn a new one.
−5. Pay yourself first.

     1. management of cash flow

     2. management of people

     3. management of personal time

6. Pay your xx well.
7. Be an "xx xx"
8. Assets buy luxuries
9. The need for reals the power of a myth
10. Teach and you shall receive

–Mortgage process – done for now
                         (put in offer xx

–Lifestyles and xx xx xx

BOAT
Break Out Another Thousand!
–computer networks xx

    –connect to server Homegroup
    (new user and xx PC's)
    –buy bigger Hard drive
    –maybe get I5 or something xx than dual core.
                Done
                Left message done
                Done Signed

250 692 386

Dr Pie

So he went to school Prom 1. Then went to university wanted to be a doctor and that is how he get his name Dr. Pie
Dr. Pie
Re ut!

Matt Pope
www.popepotluck.com
6047477323 BBS Play Time Botique
Did this for Dr. Pepper

Youtube Video
Brixley Bowd on financial collapse (green span)
778 883 5586
Vianury
Subway
Waterfall
Mon 8 2017
May

Corel Video

X10 UU20R22 – V6U7AFK
H42FUW4 – BWJPSVW
New
NBAEALL – 53RS – NRQW – J03V – 2JCWDT41
Aftershot
ALD3B22 – J4M2ZEW – HXTRNBN – MFG54V2

Alex

Invis Mortgage
604 722 0203
Aucmu.exe

515 Audio
ALCXDM – 545

Tanya-slingsby@vancity.com
1 877 811 1614
Brac general@BCCALOOP

Kate McShea Video #1

Solution #1 Person to Person Method
          Meet up groups
          Social Media

Solution #2 Rapid Sales and Enrollment Method
          Home Parties
          Trade Shows
          Live Event

Facebook	Video #2
#1 Invite	20 people
#2 Host the event	9 show up
#3 Close sales	2 sales

#1   The Big Promise Exercise

#3   Big Promise Questions
    1. Kind of People a list
    2. What are their pains/struggles/fears
    3. Biggest desires/dreams

How to _____without _____?
       Dream/desire   struggle/pain

       –Case Study as a story to share
       –Share to hold yourself accountable

    5) Boost your post
    Private message on posts.
    –Send an email to get the word out
    Video 3

    PSAEM Part II
    –Starts to hosting a successful event

-Engaging Introduction
    –Your Big Promise
    –3 questions for feeling into the future
    –everyone loves an underdog

    My Life Now
Focus on your attendees and how you make them feel.
KateMcShea.com/60min – go

Video 4

–60 minute enrollment method

1) Craft your killer offer
   Position your offer
2) Mass show upsystem
   Rinse and repeat system
3) Rapid invite formula
   –High quality prospects
   Where to find
4) Hosting event
   Relate rapid andcle method
5) Follow up surge and sales method
   –Follow up strategy

Bonus

1

Facebook live event.

2

Ad Swipe Copy Pro

3

2 Free General Admission
Raise of Freedom Summit in Phoenix Az 97 deposit

4

2917 support in Facebook group

5

Free one on one coaching call.

6

Year Membership

Bonus

1

Team Growth Formula
        –live training

2

5 live implememtation and Accountability meetings with Kate

3

Profit Automation

4

60 min Auto enrollment method

5

14 day online event launch

Value $3670
$297.00 US or three payments of 117 plus six extra

My name may have been entered twice in the draw if you put my name in
Matt Pope
604 399 9125

604 885 5453

604 886 2823 Gibsons
06/03/2017 10:00

June 3 2017

Please enter the following people in the tool Boxdream

David Carpenter	604 999 6153
Trent Gettling	604 375 6836
Bruce Armstrong	604 886 9644
Matt Pope	604 399 9125
Carey Rumba	604 863 0268
Chris at pxott Forms	

Thank You

Sorry ... you need to come in to the store and enjoy free food/music &
discounts to enter the draw

Coast's Gnarliest Tree
Photo Contest

The Local Weekly and Elphinstone Logging Focus (ELF) have partnered for an exciting photo contest.

With our unique hiking trails, you or your family have a chance to win by submitting your photo of the 'Gnarliest Tree' you can find on the Sunshine Coast!

The Sunshine Coast is blessed with a unique forest ecosystem with parts of the original forest still available to access. ELF is part of a growing movement across the Province to cherish unique stands of these older forests, along with hikers who like to roam these forests looking for rare and interesting trees. This is called 'Tree Searching'. In that spirit, ELF is hosting a photo contest to look for the 'gnarliest' tree possible as an example of the diversity of natural forms. Types of gnarly trees can include strange or surreal bark patterns, multiple trunks or woven branch structures, blown over root bases, damaged sections that have re-grown creating imaginative faces, etc.

ELF has found an example of one gnarly tree shown here in an undisclosed location in the proposed Elphinstone Park expansion area. It will not be part of the contest, however in late September we will be announcing a public walk to see this incredible example.

Send your submission to the Local editor (editor@thelocalweekly. ca) up until August 31. The judge of the 'Coast's Gnarliest Tree' will be local sculptor Rob Studer who brings a trained eye for shape and form to the contest. First prize is a cash amount of $250, second prize: a guided walk for 2 by ELF to the Roberts Creek Ancient Headwaters (lunch provided), third prize: a 2017-18 ELF supporter package: ELF

T-Shirt, Health Trail map, and Dakota Bear Sanctuary poster. The winning tree photos and photographers will be announced and featured in the Local Weekly the first week of September.

ELF has found an example of one gnarly tree shown here in an undisclosed location in the proposed Elphinstone Park expansion area. It will not be part of the contest

MATTHEW POPE

12 nights
Tokyo Day Surfing
4,000
Christ church 5500
Lifestyles 12 nights
Surfing

Tony Fowler
Spark?

Mosiac Store
Kathy on store to sell stuff
The book
The Dolphin Way
Locus – main place where something vagueness happens
Altruis control of heart & lungs and digestive tract!
Feelings and behavior to help other people and lack of self xxx
26763407   8852553

Dear Purel in the Clubhouse UK

My name is Matt at the Arrowhead clubhouse in Sechelt B.C. I have dual citizenship with the UK. Am interested in staying in the UK for awhile. Milton Keynes has been my homebase since my man was alive. I have family in London viewing a name from Canada that is payable in the UK. There would be a need to set up accommodation, arrange xxx breakfast. I xx should have xx into Milton Keynes council xx plan be a year and a let in my twenties when I worked at the middle school. Corey Rumba is the manager here in Sechelt.

Sincerely,
Matt Pope
604 399 9125 (mobile)
Dusfouas.com
BCHealthmart.com
Arrowhead-clubhouse.org
Popepotluck.com

Eric Worre

5 Strategies for Cracking the code on Social Media

–Word of mouth advertising, educating

–Build a team

–Work with our leadership

Productivity

–Social media attract and educate

–look for similar like you

Tip 1

Identify your passions outside of business

     –design

     –cooking

     –computer/Artwork

     –bikes

     –Parenting

Tip 2

Friends first

Business second

Tip 3

Be your best self

Avoid cussing

limit crowd

Networkingpro.com/socialmedia
Need course?
$297 1 hour
497 later   ebay Paypal   fax
with no   Australia
two extra bonuses   61299314888

Tip 4
Time Management
—Be social on purpose
—Couple hours of reflects
—Speaking or investing time
—Drive your agenda, not someone else's agenda

Tip #5
Don't spam create curiousity

Tip #6
Thou shalt not be boring
          Bigger than life, be interesting

Tip #7
Decide you're going to do it. Plan No Reverse

July 3, 2017
melissa@999designdeals.com
-$10.00 USD
Money Sent

Paid with   Sent to

VISA x-8540
melissa@999designdeals.com
You'll see "PAYPAL "MELISSA" on your card
Statement. Note to melissa@999designdeals.com
Part downpayment
Exchange rate
$13.40 CAD = $10.00 USD   **Details**
1 CAD = 0.75 USD   Sent to
melissa@999designdeals.com $10.00 USD

Total   **$10.00 USD**
Ship to
Matt Pope
po box 732   **Need help?**
#2-5555 periwinkle lane
If there's a problem, make sure to contact the seller
Sechelt British Columbia v0n3a0
through PayPal by **December 30, 2017.**
Canada

Transaction ID
4DK00832RW634152
payment made for new look!!

Ministry of Social Development & Social Innovation

BRITISH   Phone: 1-866-866-0800
COLUMBIA   Fax: 1-855-771-8775

Date: July 12, 2017   2 Total # of Pages
                               (includes cover page)
ATTENTION:
          Fax # 604 – 740 – 4898

We are unable to verify this person is in receipt of, or in the process of applying for income Assistance, therefore we cannot process your request at this time.

In future, please have your client confirm they are in receipt of Income Assistance prior to making your request with us by having your client call us s at 1-866-8600-0800 to get their Case ID number.

ONLY ONE PERSON PER ENQUIRY
FOR CONFIDENTIALITY PURPOSES

Thank you.

THIS MESSAGE IS INTENDED ONLY FOR THE USE OF THE INDIVIDUAL OR ENTITY TO WHICH IT IS TO ADDRESSED AND MAY CONTAIN INFORMATION THAT IS PRIVILEGED, CONFIDENTIAL AND EXEMPT FROM DISCLOSURE.

ATTN Tony Fowler;

Currently looking into expanding into New Zealand with www.
popepotluck.com. Being a UK National, this will give me the ability
to work in New Zealand or visit for extended period of times. In Canada
at the moment, would have to run resources.

Sincerely

Matthew Pope
Mobile +1 604 3999125
BBS +1 604 7472373
Fax +1 604 7404898
Email mtffxxxxx@gmail.com

64 800 800 248

Dear Council Members,

I really appreciate the time I was in Dawson City of May 1998. Seeing the view xx lie church on it was stunning. The help I had from the community the time was there was memorable. Learning a few things along the way.

Thank you.
Matthew Pope
Fax +1 604 740 4898
BBS +1 604 747 2373
Cell Mobile +1 604 3999125
www.popepotluck.com
www.BCHealthmart.com

867 993 7434
Dawson City
Office Fax
867 668 3511 Whitehorse
BOS. Centre
Fax

Dear Council Members,

I really appreciate the time being living and working in Milton Keynes for the past 20 years. The outreach love from the community has been wonderful throughout the years having some difference at times, growing as a result.

Thank you.
Matthew Pope
Fax +1 604 740 4898
BBS +1 604 747 2373
Mobile +1 604 3999125
Email mtffxxxxx@gmail.com
        mrsp57@outlook.com
www.popepotluck.com
www.BCHealthmart.com

Thx!!

Play Time Boutique has been up for almost a year. You can check our listing on BBScorner.com. The landline # is +1 6047472373. There are ten issues so far, not much. Being used with other ideas of BCHealthmart. com and Popepotluck.com.
Clubhouse International

Thank you
Sincerely

Matt Pope
Mobile +1 604 3999125
Fax +1 604 740 4898
     +44 2073795
     2369

604 595 4080
5105

ICICI

604 595 4083

Website
300 US
386.74 CDN
999designdeals

Aug 8 2017

Dear Client Service Agent,

My name is Matthew Pope. I had an account with HBC (Acct # 6002922496403490), where I paid premiums for accident insurance with you guys. Xx filing a claim while a just after leaving Sechelt, where I injured my back after a few years of heavy lifting between the years of 2008 – 2011 – 2012. My doctor is at the Sechelt clinic on Inlet Ave. in B.C. any help on this matter would greatly be appreciated.

Sincerely

Matthew Pope
Mobile 604 3999125
1 800 2598947

Xcel Men's Xplorer Fullsuit 4/3

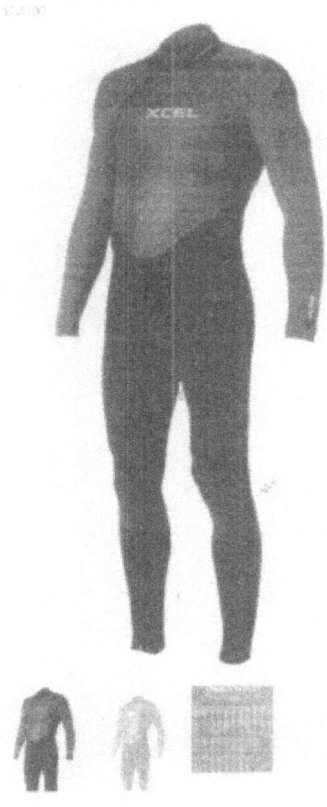

Xcel Men's Xplorer Fullsuit 4/3

$220.00

SIZE

DESCRIPTION

Entry System

OS

Smarter offset ("OS") back entry design keeps the zipper off the spine to reduce pressure and increase flexibility and comfort; with glued and blindstitched zipper flaps and a reinforce zipper base.

Materials

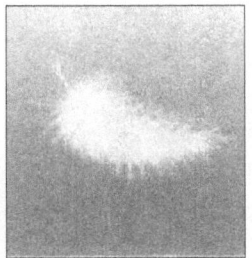

Ultrastretch Neoprene

Comfortable, lightweight neoprene with softer foam and a tighter weave textile for less water absorption and better durability.

Texture Skin

Texture embossed rubber that provides excellent wind resistance, ideal for outer chest panels hoods, and other areas that would otherwise lose warmth quickly.

Construction

Glued & Blindstitched Seams

A fully sealed, maximum stretch seam construction that keeps water out. Neoprene panels are glued and pressed together, then blindstitched (needle doesn't fully penetrate neoprene, keeping WATER OUT).

Fit

http://switchbladesurf.com/product/xcel-mens-xplorer-4-3/ Xcel Men's Xplorer Fulisuit 4/3 | Custom Surfboards, Ding Repair, Wetsuits & Surf Acce... Page 3 of 4

Smarter product design means minimizing seams to maximize stretch. Any seams used are always pre bent and contoured for a truly engineered fit.

Dura Flex Knee Panels

DuraFlex Knee Panels

Contoured, durable panels that stretch with you.

RELATED PRODUCTS

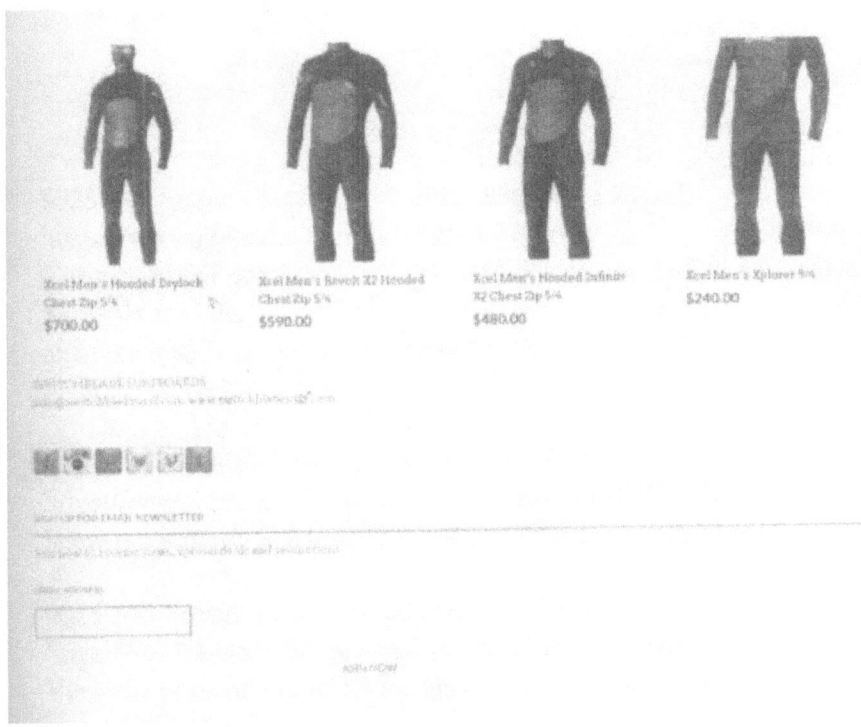

Xcel Men's Hooded Drylock Chest Zip 5/4
$700.00

Xcel Men's Revolt X2 Hooded Chest Zip 5/4
$590.00

Xcel Men's Hooded Infiniti X2 Chest Zip 5/4
$480.00

Xcel Men's Xplorer 9/4
$240.00

http://switchbladesurf.com/product/xcel-mens-xplorer-4-3/8/9/2017

Job Fair
Sept 16 #
15
CMk?
Bedford University in MK.

The Orange
Asian restaurant

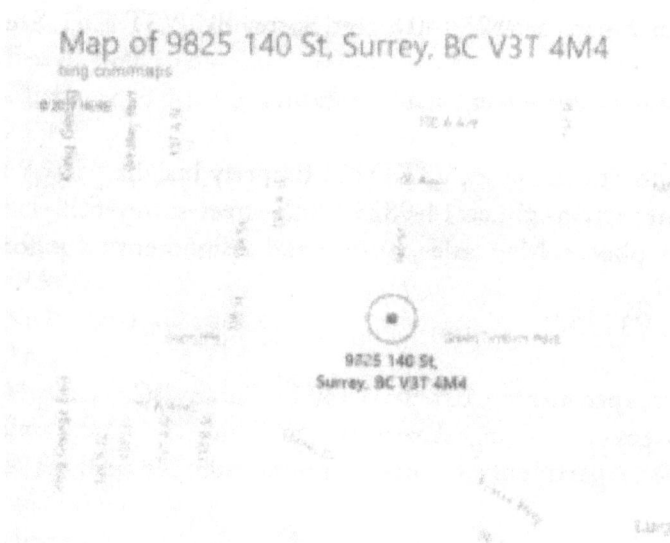

9825 140 Street - Surrey - For Sale? Ask Us - Lilypad
https://www.lilypad.ca/surrey/9825-140-street
Contact one of our agents at (604) 330-012 to see if 9825 140 Street,
Surrey is for sale,
or to see nearby homes in the neighbourhood!

#219 - 9825 140 ST, SURREY, BC | RE/MAX
https://www.remax.ca/bc/surrey-real-estate/219-9825-140-st-8371885
View property details for 9825 140 in SURREY | RE/MAX

9825 140 Street, Surrey | Sold? Ask us - Zolo.ca
https://www.zolo.ca/surrey-real-estate/9825-140-street
View the price of real estate in this neighbourhood. see homes for sale
near 9825 140
Street, Surrey. or learn if this home is for sale today!

9825 140 Street, Surrey BC - Walk Score
https://www.walkscore.com/score/9825-140-st-surrey-bc-canada
View photos and maps of 9825 140 Street, Surrey BC, V3T 5M1.
See the Walk Score or Share a 2bedroom independent apartment! June

14 - 9825 140th Street, Surrey, V3T5M1 | Property Insight
https:/www.propertyinsight.ca/14-9825.140th-street-surrey-bc...
Find property photos. Map, sales, history and assignment value for
14 – 9825 140th
Street. Surrey. V3T5M1

Green Timber Apartments - 109-9825 140 St, Surrey, BC
www.yellowpages.ca. Lodging>Apartments near me
Green Timber Apartments - Surrey - phone number. website & address
BC. –
Apartments

9825 140 Street, Surrey, BC V3T 5M1 - allhx.ca
www.allhx.ca/bc/surrey/140-street/9825
Transit options, nearby parks & school for 9825 140 Street, Surrey

1 9825 140 St Surrey - Snap Up Real Estate
https://www.snapuprealestate.ca/property/Surrey-BC/1-9825 140-St
Property info for 1 9825 140 St in the No Neighbourhood neighbourhood
of Surrey

Root Computer Services 9825 140 St, Surrey, BC
www.yellowpages.ca Internet | Internet Consultants near me
Root Computer Services - Surrey phone number. Website & address-
BC - Internet
Consultants.

9825 - 9825 140 ST, Surrey - Canada Postal Codes
https://www.canadapostalcodes.net/ /surrey/140-st/9825 9825

Bed & Bathe
Chef's
74.99 ?
69.99 ?
Set 49.99
frying pan
49.99
No bottle or oil needed
And
Meal replacement
Bars 3.99
20 for Heath
Mix for men or
Women

T & T
45.99 – flat pot with strainer steamer
Snacks for 2.99/3.99
Barley tea 3.99
Round eyesteak 4.19
Pork chops thin cut 2.80 – 5.50?
Drinks like vitamin water or ca? 1.99
Virgin
Phone prepaid outright
99.99 – 89.99
Brick Sechoal   998 tent sale
Pillow top mattress
Sleep country downtown
Mattress 700, plan 70.00/month
Kiwis market
Grapes red or green bag 2.50

Inconcebles

CSM.CA@ICICIDARK.com

Aug 10 2017

TO PAM & HOWARD

Heard they split, but if they go ahead on the 12th best of luck both ways.

Matt Insert MP_Image 015

Matt

Internet Domain Name Service Inc.
2900 Warden Avenue
Box #92090
Toronto, Ontario M1W 3Y8

Domain Name Expiration Notice
visit us at www.idns.ae

A **courtesy** to domain name holders, we are sending you this notification of the domain name registration that is due to expire in the next few months. When you switch today to Internet Domain Name Services, you can take advantage of our best savings. Your registration for: **popepotluck.com** will expire on **November 22, 2017**. Act today!

Domain name: popepotluck.com
Reply Requested By: August 28, 2017

You must renew your domain name to retain exclusive rights to it on the Web, and now is the time to transfer and renew your name from your current Registrar to Internet Domain Name Services. Failure to renew your domain name by the expiration date may result in a loss of your online identity making it difficult for your customers and friends to locate you on the Web.

Privatization of Domain Registrations and Renewals now allows the consumer the choice of Registrars when initially registering and also when renewing a domain name. Domain name holders are not obligated to renew their domain name with their current Registrar or with Internet Domain Name Services. Review our prices and decide for yourself. You are under no obligation to pay the amounts stated below, unless you accept this offer. **This notice is not a bill**, it is rather an easy means of payment should you decide to switch your domain name registration to Internet Domain Name Services.

Term Period covered		Price
1 year	Until -- Nov 22, 2018	$40.00
2 years (Recommended)	Until Nov 22, 2019	$70.00 (save $10)
5 years (Best Value)	Until -- Nov 22, 2022	$160.00 (save $40)

The following names are currently available for you to register and secure, protecting your domain name from being duplicated.

Available Domains	Period covered	Price
popepotluck.net	2 Years	$70.00 *
popepotluck.org	2 Years	$70.00 *

For a complete list of our terms and conditions, please visit www. idns.ae/tos

Transfer and renew your domain name online at **www.idns.ae** 24 hours a day, 7 days a week.

Please detach this stub and include it with your payment.

Check the appropriate boxes of the Domain Names you would like to order.

popepotluck.com

Expiration Date	Reply Requested By	Renewal Term	Payment
		1 Year	$40.00
November 22, 2017	August 28, 2017	2 Year	$70.00
		5 Year	$160.00

Available Domain Names (Optional)

Popepotluck.net

1 Year $40.00*

2 Year $70.00*

5 Year $160.00*

popepotluck.org

1 Year $40.00*

2 Year $70.00*

5 Year $160.00*

(*Please add GST)

Total Amount_____

If paying by credit card, please enter your information below:

Card Number:

MATT POPE BCHEALTHMART INC.
PO BOX 732
SECHELT BC V0N 3A0

_____

Please provide a valid email address on the above line

Matt Pope <mtffxxxxx@gmail.com>

Receipt From Online Leadership Pro, LLC
1 message

Kristine Marifosque <kris@katemcshea.com>
Tue, Aug 29, 2017 at 5:05 PM
To: mtffxxxxx@gmail.com

Receipt From Online Leadership Pro, LLC
Paid $80.00
Invoice #12789

MATTHEW POPE

Data Entry

Module Section 30w Page Optimization

Long tail — more specific keywords

Short tail — brief keywords

Offline research

Customer

Online Key Phrases

Key terms who, what, whose and why

Tread, Volume

Favoor (website) unique sites search vouchers

Written cow teat terms

(keyword search (bolo text))

Module section 4 – off page optimization

- -links/ social media
- -one way links more authority
- -Inbound links, positive profile, relevance, authority, anchor text to our site
- -request google to remove links
- -Domain authority in boosting links
- -Low spam score
- -reach out to websites give you links to links on your site (keyword rich)
- Content marketing

- Outreach (……..) create relevant (….) content. Media, bloggers
- Social links Facebook, Youtube, Google+ Social page linked to your site (keyword rich) organic Google+
- Module section 5 Analysis and case study
- Tools Criteria KPIs
- Quality of traffic overall better organic visibility
- Google search console for
- Baseline create a benchmark (…..) Analyze and review.
- Get stat ranking report
  - KPIs
  - Visibility, Engagement, organic traffic, quality traffic
  - KPIs
  - Mainly conversations
  - Engagement (….. goal)
  - Visibility of your brand
  - Laces and guidelines
  - (……) notice
  - Privacy and data collections
  - Credit a service

○ Accessibility for everyone to ease

Module 3 setting goals

Max CPC pay x Adwords ranting dorm

Key word relevance (quality) score = rank

Click thru vote = higher likes?

- Step 1 what are your business objectives
- Step 2 develop goals for each business objective
- Step 3 Identify your KPIs metrics
- Step 4 Identify targets (numerical values)
- PPC KPIs (Key Performance Indicators)
- Direct response
- Conversions
- Cost per conversion
- Bonuses on vote

- Awareness (Branding)
- Average position (metrics)
- Click thru rate
- Cost per click
- Engagement
- Click through vote conversions (pdf documents)
- Web analysis metrics
- Create google adwords account (google.com/adwords)
- Implement keyword research
- Conversion – set budgets
- Tracking/ impact choose targeting options

- Analytics goals – establish campaign architecture
- Launch campaign create ad copy
- Define landing page
- Establish bidding structure

- Module 3
- Campaign setup structure
- Configure language
- Geographic targeting
- Budget campaigns caster multiple ad groups
- Ad group
- Group ads be quality and or subject configure
- CPC groups
- Ad group keyword
- Ad groups center suite
- Own keywords and ads
- Set as ad group or keyword level
- Search meters only
- Search meters with display sheet
- Display websites only
- Shopping
- Video on Youtube
- Universal App campaign

- Targeting
- List sites manually
- Device setup
- Bids and budget
- 20% more than daily budget within year contract

- How much you invest to pay per click
- Keywords
- Valuable and appropriate
- Search terms to target
- DMI principle because of select information is available to creditors
- Tools
- Google-TRENDS.com

- Key word planner
- List of keywords
- Choose target search
- Put in website
- Clues glue reading ad plan enter manually average cost.
- Keyword match types
- Exact match
- Please match
- Broad match modifier
- Broad match for starting campaign
- Negotiate searches

Module 3 search marketing

PPC Pay per click

Process

1. Goals, search setup, adsearch, quality score
2. Setup Keyword search, ad copy, targeting delivery
3. Manage adcentre reports goal tracking

4. Analyze analysis tools, KPIs, Review
- SeM Search engine marketing when to offer PPC
- Use PPC to fill in the graph where organizations was
- Enhance visibility
- Get immediate and early access to the market
- Customize messaging board on users specifications.

- Search engine strategy which and terms
- Positioning
- Google knowledge graph (search results)
- SEO PPC work together (adwords)
- PPC Common terms
- Paid search cost per click (CPC)
- SEM click through rate (CTR)

- Module 3 Ad Copy
- Best practices
  - Compelling message – USP
  - Match ad to landing page
  - Highlight call to action
  - Create mobile specific ads where relevant
  - Promotions and offers – Discount
  - Free, limited offer – amount of
  - Include keywords in AD carry left. Create urgency

- Ad Copy: Composition
- Ad title 125 Characters
- Description 1: 35 characters
- Description 2: 35 characters
- Display URL
- Domain needs to be the name a friend URL
- Rules
- Character limits do not exceed

- Limitations of special characters excessive punctuation and capitalization.
- Do not use word click trademark of terms in ADcopy is restricted.
- No misrepresentation of false representation a product or service.
- Display URL must accurately reflect the landing page / destructed URL
- Ads tab creation of Adwords interface 2 – 3 ads per ad group
- Trial multiple ads
  - Different wording
  - Different call to
  - Different landing page
- Dynamic keyword insertion

- Ad extensions (free)
- Call out extensions
- Structured snippet
- Site links
- ASOS – do a search

- Creative site live extensions ad eccentrics tab.
- Landing pages
- Decision in 8 seconds
- F. View theory (need more on left) above the fold award scrolling
  - Landing pages
- Provides relevant useful and original content
- Transparent and trust
- Easy to wave gate
- Content matches search query

- Fulfills the promise from the referral source
- Product, title and emerge prominent and risible
- Clear calls to action
- Minimal clicks to commission (less than 3 is the rule of thumb)

- Module 3 Google Display Network
- AdSense
- For every 1000 then pay ; free after itself
  - Remarketing and RLSA
  - YouTube, etc. Audiences
- Frequency cap (stop showing ads)
- Incentivize them to come back (AdSense ate 20%)
  - Audience list
- Mobile app, customer email, YouTube, website

- ○ Website
- Implementing a tag on website under audiences tab, use your own email address to person doing
  - ○ Code AdSense
- Link YouTube and AdSense
- SOK Apps
- Email customer match exceed and YouTube from om database plead

- Manage
- Beds and Budgets
- Set budget at creation stage
- Adgroup level (A mending bed) default bed except one case
- Adgroup tab
- Keyword level set piece per CPC
- Amending budgets
- Settee tale
- KPIs
- Increase budget for keywords / adgroup that perform well
- Decrease budget keywords / adgroups not doing well against KPIs

- Adwords Interface
- Campaign, adgroups, setups, ads always show.
- Opportunities tab go to realign a beguine

- Module 3 Conversion Tracking
- Basics

- Post click success of your campaign if your investment is generating a letter
  - ○ Adwords conversion tracking code
  - ○ Impact google analytics
- Analytics for comparison
- Conversion teaching google adwords
- Tools – conversions
- Click on website
- Inquire a call – purchases/ conversion per click
- Main 30days shopping
- Conversion teaching – google analytics
- From previous 14 days activity
- Launch adwords - analytics

Adwords

Analyze

Repeating

-Campaign, adgroup and keyword performance

-Download and schedule

-Dimensions

-Filters

-Columns

-Respect editor

Click download

Select file

-By time network, day, time, device

-can choose to schedule

-Dimensions

Dimensions tab view live on conversion type

-columns

-adgroups tab

Colums section (modify columns)

Filters

Filter Id

-allows you to better data customized to your business

-can do line

Adwords respect editor

Basic – Campaign

Google analytics setting KPIs

- Copyright- Define Business/ Website objectives
- DMCA- Develop your KPIs that digital will increase success
- Millennium- analyze marketing activities
- Copy write action new campaign ad and further content marketing
- PPC reason measure results-
- Searchenginelaid.com
- Analyze year KPIs
- Data protection
- For only noted purposes
- Collect on cookie data

- Module 5
- Delivery/ Management
- Schedules
- Send tues or thurs
- Open 10am – 12pm

- Emails 2pm – 4pm
- Business to consumer
- Open time vary by industry
- Module 5
- Reporting and analysis

Reporting

- Open rate
- Total opens
- Image opens
- Clicks
- Unsubscribes
- On mobile device allow between images and text.
- Boarded
- Delivered reporting
- Recipient activity
- Link activity
- Campaign snapshot dashboard report

- Module 5
- Laws and guidelines
- Data Protection Regulations
- Be aware of what is considered as spam
- Privacy Regulations
- Know common characteristics of electronic privacy regulation

Recap

- Start
- Use a service
- Build your list

- Design – respect your etiquette brand and audience
- Always look at experts
- Integrate
- Iterate
- Social sharing and forwards

Split testing

- Sender (name best response)
- Subject (timeline and relevance of messaging.
- Content

Concerns and interests

Advantage of subscriber's better information

- Can reveal a significant level of difference between companies
- Split testing can greatly improve the success of email campaigns.

- Module 6 Introduction Social media
- Collection Websites and applications
- Social media marketing
- The process of gaining traffic, attention and interaction with customers thru social media to drive directive indirect sales
- Crowd aimed and paid
- Engagement from community
- Sharing
- Interacting
- Customers social communities
- Community followers on twitter

- Publishing
- Blog
- Website
- Advertising
- Targeting
- Paying to reach exactly right sentences

Emergency platforms

- Xing professional network in Germany (similar to linkedin)
- QQ- Desktop Messenger service in china (owned by tencent)
- Wechat- mobile messenger service agreement
- Weilo – microblogging service in china hybrid of facebook and twitter (tencent)

VR paperless Russian social networker service

Google analytics mosaic collective tab

-turn on remarketing for properties

-For properties advertising repeating features

Import to adword

Ad extension google tag area in chrome to get website data property data

1 head right click source code

Closing header code or lag

UA to see if joint to overview c-rep analytics account master view

Module 4 Digital display advertising

Homepage takeover

Handover takeover border mid placement in uaichile of page

- Ad impression one takeover majority of time
- Hyperlink banner 'live link'
- In stream digital display advertisement
- Social media advertising.

Module 4 display advertising Industry Overview

- Moving up a little
- more toward mobile devices
- real time bidding
- Ad impression
- arrival user arriving after an ad banner being exposed
- Ad unique user consumer of ad content determined by unique device

Module 4 Terminology and mechanism

- ad click click on ad impression
- Ad impression # of ad banner being served
- click measurement of a mouse click on a hyperlink
- completed download request for a site, used or live, file transfer greater than 95%

- cookie text file on hardware to remember websites user data

- digital display advertising display adverts appearing on webpages

Terminology

- Geographical IP
  Analysis percentages of countries established for a given metric such as unique users
- HTML hypertext markup language
- keyword words or phrases to trigger your ad to appear
- page impression request or for a page of a sites content
- rich media interactive media
- flash impression total number of pages requests made for pages
- visit user engages in a single burst of energy
  o DDA Stakeholders
    • Advertisers
    • Agencies
    • Publishers
    • Audience
  o Criteria for publishers
    • Mechanics, Advertiser,
    • publisher website, customer, advertiser
  o Real-time bidding
    • Matching ad impression + (pairing at inventory and data)
  o Module 4 Benefits and challenges
  o Business value

- Control targeting and measurement capabilities
- User response ability to generate clicks
  - Integration (Online)
    - Integrates with other aspects of the digital marketing mix.
  - Integration (offline) with campaigns
  - The Powel
    - Awareness
    - Consideration
    - Intent
  - Displays its purchase
    - Support
    - Loyalty
    - Advocacy
  - Marketing benefits
    - Teach—Awareness— Branding
    - Influence
  - Full transparency
    - Continuity and consistency even with offline media access messaging
  - C+R click thru rates
    - Range from 0.1-0.3% Branding
  - Display ad 50% made a purchase
  - Video less than 30 secs
    - Post impression takes

action on decision making think clearly substantiated
  - Floating ads
    - Move cursor over ad
  - Expandable ads
    - Increase in size cost to get metrics eight
  - Rich media contains streaming
    - Video within the ad
    - Animated built in video
  - Road blocks
    - Tandem ads
  - Smart banner works within ad lanner
  - Branding
  - Static ads
  - Formats
    - Animation
  - Film strip
    - Content rich
    - Contains fine ads
    - Users can explore
  - Emerging mobile formats
  - Filmstrip
  - Slider
  - Adhesion
  - Full page
  - Push banner
  - Facebook and Twitter will take 33% of US market share
  - 65% of Twitter ad revenue

is from mobile tablets and smart phones
- ○ LinkedIn target is job title
- ○ Instagram imager
- ○ Module 4 6A campaign process
  - • Target audience
    - • Demographics
    - • Geography
    - • Interests
    - • Consumers leave a trail
      - ○ Browse
        - – click
        - – register
        - – Buy

- • Matching audiences to publishers
  - • Relevance
  - • Google display planner in AdWords tools and analysis menu
  - • Keep it short
    - ○ Interactivity scale
  - • Conversion
  - • Direct response
  - • Engagement
  - • Awareness and branding

- • Smart objectives
  - • Specific
  - • Measurable
  - • Actionable
  - • Realistic

- • Timed
- • 0.1 percent click rate

- • Module 4 formats
  - ○ Campaign budget
    - • Budgeting factors
  - ○ Target audience
  - ○ Segmentation
  - ○ Publisher/ website price
  - ○ Paints
  - ○ Geography – multi-rational sites cost to make
  - ○ Competition
  - ○ Cost of Creative
    - • Cost more expandable banners
  - ○ CPM (cost per minute)
    - • Most expensive
  - ○ CPC (Cost Per Click)
  - ○ CPL (Cost Per Lead)
    - • Smart banner
  - ○ CPA (Cost per Acquisition)
    - • filling submission form
  - ○ tenciviy / sponsor
    - • Call to action email
    - • Book time
      - • Fixed amount
  - ○ Calculate cost
  - ○ Cost per mile
  - ○ Per 1000 ad impressions
  - ○ No. of impressions
  - ○ 1000

- ○ Google owns 33% of online media marketing
  - • Use an agency
- ○ Google display network
- ○ Ad Copy
  - • Clear call to action (CTA)
  - • Strong design (Fit for format)
- ○ Content sensitive copy
  - • (user and publisher)
- ○ Copy informed by keyword search
- ○ Brand prominence
- ○ Direct and concise language
- ○ Use of Imperative
- ○ Split testing
- ○ Factors based on
  - • Creative
  - • Text
  - • Call to action
    - • Advantages of Split testing
  - • Better interaction and conversion rates
  - • More targeted and relevant content
  - • Better ROI
    1. Content
    2. Offer
    3. Pricing
    4. Creative
    5. Call to action
    6. Banner size

-cap number of times at 5 that is shown to a unique user.

Campaign targeting

-contextual targeting

-Behavioral targeting

Retargeting

Remarketing types

-Standard – visited sites

-Dynamic – visited products

-Mobile visit via mobile

-Search – search ads

-video – watched your videos

How to track and monitor ROI

-the publisher, sales and network

-Internal analytics and reporting

-any offline reports and measures

Reports should include

# of empressions

# of clicks

-Clicks thru rate

-Conversions

Double click by google

Module 4

Laws and guidelines

-Privacy

-Data protection

-Copyright – stock photos ask permissions

-Accessibility

AAP.org

Module 5

Into Email marketing

Subscriber management

-content and design

-revenue generator

Higher click rate

-structured systematic process

Emarketer.com

3 times as many email accounts as facebook and twitter combined 66% made a purchase of Email marketing 20% via facebook

Email service provider A hosted cloud based email marketing system

Advantage of Email services order

No hardware

Woman's serve

Whitelist allows messages to be received.

Blacklist Block lists

Low cost of entry

High level of functionality and reporting.

Module 5

Email Marketing Process

-Spam means "Unsolicited Bulk Email"

-Send emails if permission given in a 12 month window

Send similar products or services

> May not send no consent in the last 12 months

-Provide email sent form

-A valid physical address at work to sender manage.

Contacted has not been provided

> Marketing rules

-Never buy lists

-Never share lists

-Never Assume

-Have process for scales (Automatic)

-Don't mix your messages

If you get it wrong

-Prove you have a process

-2000 was for email

Module 5

Subscriber management

1. Data collection

2. Data segmentation

3. Data management

> Your lists

-Bigger list = greater success

-Pay attention to subscriber sources

-Segmentation

-Business systems and form capture

-Focus on quality – not quantity

-How does regulator apply?

> Data collection: online

> Email subscription not on home page

-sign up forms (less Intrusive)

Different levels of No

-Don't fit at this time

-Budget not at this time

-Old customer

-Too expensive

-Already got a supply

Offline

-Conferences and events

-any meeting point

Segmentation

Forget emails have same needs and wants

-Demographic

-Geography

-History

-Relationship

-Stage in Life cycle

-subscription after purchase

-visits website

-link activity

-shares topic

-likes on facebook

Link activity based on interaction # of clicks (KPI)

Prospects

Lapsed or dorment customer.

Data management

Clean old data regular

Smaller amount of itself

Apply Segmentation Consistently

-Update information with customers

-Every iteration of Email marketing process is an opportunity to ensure data coding

Module 5 Newsletter Content and Design

User prioritization

Exercise

From name subject line message review

Risks

-relevance of the message

-Frequency of sending

-Interruption factor

Sender

Cultural bias, gender bias depending on from name

"From Name" should be from "read" reply

-Allow recipient to reply

Subscriber Prioritization Criteria

-time of day

-when email sent/ received

-Location (user and sender)

-Sender Familiarity

-Work Priorities

-Personal Priorities

Subject Line

-First 2 or 3 words are crucial

-Make subject line relevant to the recipient as opposed to the sender

-Subject lines are industry dependent

-test, test, test (split testing)

Email Copy

Structured for ease of consumption / scanning

-Headline

-Paragraph headings

-Bullet points

-bold text

-text/ image balance

-links

-Avoid too much text

Attachments

-try not to use them

Images

-Use alt text email messages

-Images should not

Carry Image incased

turned off (Images) 44 dollar return for every

dollar spent.

-limits call to action on mobile devices

Interaction evolution

-traditional marketing broadcast

-Digital marketing targeted niche marketing

Interaction level

Lightweight

like

follow

click link

Medium

comment

reply

endorsements

Enter contest

Highly engaged

Share

Retweet

Review

Recommendation

Transact

Register

Subscribe

Purchase

Module 6 social listening

Identifying and assessing about what we said about you.

Customers

Understand

challenges

Competitors

Products

Services

Industry

Follow and Encourage with marketers

Listening tools

-social mention

-google alerts – in general

-twazzop – twitter

-klout it as well you are doing on social media

Customer and Influencer identification

-Understand your community

-Identify Influencers across twitter, Facebook, YouTube, etc.

-who – it is followers #'s

high activity – High engagement

-What thought leaders, Bloggers

-How create connection build relationships

-case study

Uniqlo partnered with fashion Blogger

-Result highest sales figures in 4 years

Balanced listening

Can be distracting to be too tuned into the market and the competitions activities.

Remember

Social listening helps you listen to

what your customers are saying your products/ services

Content planning

Plan

> Align with other marketing activities

Manage

> Leverage all tools available to be efficient

Adapt

Balance between planned activity and real time activity

> Content schedule with updates

Timing of updates

-time of day and week

-goal of update

> Social networks for specific updates

-twitter, Facebook, LinkdIn, Youtube views

Format

Video 30 secs

Publishing

-conversational

(make 90 words count)

-Ask questions

-Story telling (voter own pics)

Business to Business

> Publishing

-Keep it human

> -Business decision makers are people on social media

> Add Value

-Inform

-Educate

-Evangelize

Story telling

-Showcase your satisfied customers via testimonials.

Make them look good (and you too)

> Content Pan

Actions, resources, time frame = Content plan

Social Media Application

-contribution in recruitment, customer service and business

> Insights

-Success will be determined by usage customer profile

Building a brand requires consistency of tone, communication, voice message, look and feel.

Social Media is extremely powerful to facilitate that in a regular lightweight environment.

Brands are build on consistency across platform- online and offline

Ensure to leave a solid social media strategy to protect against reputation risks and ensuring plans are in place to handle negative commentary completely.

Social media in business

-For best results its critical to secure budget and resources.

-Acknowledge personal is public

-drives more actionable outcomes

Goal setting for social

Goals for social can be broad be selective about your primary goals.

Module 6 Facebook

-Personal vs Business max 5000 connections

-Keep videos short as possible 1 min max

-long videos a series 4567

Developers facebook.com

Like button

Send button

Comments box

Activity feed

Recommendations

Hashtags- links

Facebook.com/Page/Create

Page posts

-Kiss- Keep it short and sweet

-include links on shared posts

-make it about customer's videos, Imagery

-Pin to top page

Keep tone positive

Facebook offers

-Create offer 1 event

-messenger for business Instant replies (up to 250 characters)

-save instant replies

Facebook Contests

-Prize should be relevant and attractive to the right audience

-craft copy and imagery sharp and to the point. Like and comment , okay share, like was not okay

Cant ask people to "tag"

Verify your page

-Page settings

-several 7 page verification

-verify this page

Phone all/ documentation

-live stream

Facebook "Events"

-In compose, select "create event" option

-create landing page

-after event add comments photos

Facebook Apps

-E-commerce (stores) done by other sources

-Service

-Booking

-Contests

-Games

Facebook Places

-Allows you to be easily found in Facebook Search

-Adjust the places if required

-Search by location

Facebook Groups

-Create communities

-Internal communications

-Deliver Complete Service

-Connect on single project or topic

Module 6 Instagram

"Instagram is a fun and quirky way to share your life with friends through a series of pictures"

Hashtags 5-10 hashtags to be more easily found

Content visual, High quality photography

Personal US Brand no difference divulge = primarily mobile device Hoot suite to post from desktop to Instagram align contests with coworker

Post

-add location

-share to facebook, twitter (as relevant)

-Include caption

-repost use an app GiFshare for eg.

High quality imagery

Consistent at voice, campaign hashtags and content planning are key to strong relationships

Module 6 Twitter

-Microblogging up to 140 characters

-Business and Personal handles are both public by default

-Promote your twitter handle cover Image/Profile Image

Follow Others

-Use search bar to find and follow leaders, brand champions, clients, competitors.

-thank for retweet

-Direct message

-Hashtags # (no more than 2 hashtags) theme or passion about event.

-link or destination no hashtags

-URL Shortening

-Advanced search = search for topics of interest to you by keyword or by people on twitter

-geotag share the location from where you tweet to make tweets richer, esp good for events

-good or bad – great way to build alliances, retweet clients to share activity to your clients to share activity to your clients be in complete agreement.

-Be proactive = follow others whose content you find most valuable for your community

-create lists to retweet list from events find out what they're talking about

Dec. twitter.com/web plugins for your site

-why cross promote

-kind of plugins embedded tweets embedded videos

Contests

-keep prize relevant to audience

-tweet multiple times vary

-Include terms and conditions

Twitter lists is a pool of twitter accounts

-private and public lists

They get notification

-private lists for potential clients not work feed.

Buzz feed

Trending on twitter

Scheduling and publishers APP

Tweet check

Hoot suite

Buffer

Additional insights

-Follower work

-socialbakers

> Tweet 3-5 times of day general rule of thumb for up to 24 hours or save.

-Periscope is to own App via twitter connected will inform watch live video broadcasts.

Module 6

-connect world's professions

-complete each section of your profile

-Include employment history

-add photos

-Amend privacy

-claim your shortened link URL

-Include 3 links to other sources

-Keep professional at all times

-Share videos Images

-showcase your expertise

-Endorse and recommend

Trusted connections in positive light Prospecting

-use advanced search features

-Personalize any in – mails to request connection

> Groups

-people connect with like minded people

-are private

-You can be a member of (max 50 groups)

-Quality vs quantity

-manage set parameters

-go to create group

-group name

-summary

> Visibility (listed or unlisted)

-website (optional)

> Publishing

-long form posts (400 words)

-Auto promoted

-Potential for viral search

-separate entity for nosiness page

-show case page can feature different product lines.

-career opportunities

> Jobs

Subscription product

-compare profiles

Recruiter

-see talent in familiar way

-create posts for new posts up to ten

> AdWords extension video party

-google my business account

-call extension button on phone

-can show on all campaign types desktops cannot make a call not linked to Skype or google phone

Call out adds extra information to your customers

-wont show on display network only campaigns

-Structured snippets list certain brands group level

-Price ext.

> Display products in price range

Helpful tips (Best practices)

-match extensions to business goals

-use multiple extensions

-remember to update ad extensions

> Module 7 Google + and Pinterest

Transfer Facebook to google + (SEO rankings)

Hangouts on Air

> Any live engagement event

> Pinterest

Digital Scrapbook

> 85% female visitor

Etsy (sell items there)

Pin in a post (upload)

Piing from site can add

Pin it button on site when

You have a business account

> Subject targeting

Buyable pins

Ability to communicate with

Specific US ecommerce

Platforms

> Rich pins

-App

-Place location

-Article location of Acticle

-Recipe gets ingredients

-movie pins pulls up reviews

Cinematic pins

Engagement when scrolling

Module 7 Google + Youtube

-google stream already photos to choose from

Discoverability

-click "share", "embed" then paste on site

> Social Sharing

-account settings

-connected accounts

-connect and Authorize twitter

-account

Consider tone of tweet

Creator studio

Channel the branding

Add a watermark branding

Add the watermark and use your logo

Save this and make it so it appears for whatever length of video you choose

Content types

Opinion

Story telling

Web viewer

Commerce

Live event

Interactive format (360/Hangout)

> Advertising

Can be controlled by AdWords

-pay for videos watched on true view

--In-stream ads play before another from a YouTube partner

-Display ads

Appear alongside other YouTube videos

-cards earned value user gets more information in video

Overlay Call ti Act row cards

-are clickable area that pop up upon a video to drive traffic to another location

-on trueview ads

YouTube targeting is simple and easy to implement

Analytics

You can see the most high level view

AdWord exts

Part 2

Click on ad extensions each site link has to lead unique page same domain

Structured snippets are for only search wetwork! Don't expect yourself

Match on your site of prices/language under extensions

Module 7

Facebook and Instagram advertising

-right hand side only desktop

-newsfeed clicked 50 times more that RHS

-Boost is not targeted

-Promoting throwing dart at earthcard

-link embed with image and call to action

-primary action – website, video

-secondary action – like, comment

-offer – make offer not offered anywhere else

Carousel

-carousel is a format that delivers a slide of 3 -5 images and links in one sequence, tell a story

Canvas

Canvas is an immersive and expensive experience on Facebook for businesses

Module 7

Facebook Advertising (Continued)

Audience Network

Is currently only a few to the following objective campaigns

-mobile Apps

Engagement ads

Website Conversion Ads

Website Click Ads

Objectives

OCPM (optimized cost per thousand) in 2014

Facebook targeting

Who do you want to target to.

Stick to lifetime budgets

Schedule Ads

Ad quality + targeting = Position and score

Campaign Structure

Campaign

Adset	Adset	Adset
Advert	Advert	Advert
Advert	Advert	Advert

Ad Manager

-look at performance

Facebook.com ads

-change delivery

-Power

Create ads in bulk campaigns

Create ads copy campaigns

Weekly reports

Conversion reports 2 a week

Daily reports for junior

Understanding the breakdown of your ads will give you insight into their performance and the responses

-Age

-gender, etc

Page Insights

-snapshot of performance

-page KPIs and ad KPIs

-How much cost per click

-referal + offer

Export Data

-page level data

-post level data live by live add is more than limit reports up to 180 days

Page to watch

-Ability to track competitors

-take with grain of salt

-spend budget correctly

Module 7 twitter

Objective based advertising CP + cost per action

Twitter engagements with a new hashtags

-twitter website card entire format is doable use a tracking

-call to action button

Ad types

Format can be used to clue decoders of

an app a to create engagement audience be app

-Format delivered in resolute bard

-Leads can be collected into simple excel lists

Leads can be linked directly to CRM so as to have rules for communications

Autoplay video only pay when servers views video

8 sec view length

Tweet engagement with 24 hour promote trend

Targeting is the backbone to any campaign create lists

-can target keywords

-interest points, sports, etc

-transmission times on twitter

Tailored audiences

Allow you to re-target

-replaced email list

-use

-website visitors felt a code snippet at face website or in a fragment.

Audience Platform

Tweet engagement campaigns on twitter became interaction and nature ads

-Promoted video campaigns

-App install a re-engagement

Analytics- expert data

Similar to Facebook- left is a rate right to pay

Measure your mentions use measurements

Module 7

LinkedIn Advertising

Analytics and IOUs

-is the audience schedule

-500 – 600 % more expensive per cost per clicks

-only after IHB Formats within their in entry (banner ads)

-professional Platform should reflect the name

-slide share- knowledge sharing available on desktop and mobile

-In mail very specific

Lead Cancellation

-Fantastic way to build a tunneling strategy

-text ads on only desktop

Social Ads

-group ads (company)

-follow page

-spotlight ads featured emplooyees

Targeting

Targeting is tailored to professional targeting

Analytics

Similar to facebook

-within Google Analytics

UTM codes, create a tag

Segment out our campaigns

Google search tools

Publishing

Essentially a blog

3rd party tools (social)

-sprout social, Facebook Power editor, Sprinklr, Hoot Suite, Brand watch

Become master of nature world first

Laws and guidelines

-Yield to common sense

-part of your ethics

Module 8

Micro moments

I want to know moments

I want to go moments

I want to do moments

I want to buy moments

2015 was tipping point for mobile devices then tablet or desktop

Few steps as possible on mobile

Fantastic targeting opportunities location specific information

Influence loop

Stimulus

1. awareness
2. consideration
3. evaluation
4. purchase
5. experience
6. loyalty
7. advocacy

Customers should be saying positive things about us

Mobile customer is 3 more times more valuable than wo mobile

Value of purchase is higher

Module 8

Mobile Optimized sites and Apps

Mobile sites

1. location
2. screen size
3. touch screen and

1. Download processing speed
2. Navigation
3. Available time

Responsive web design

Adaptive web design

Avoid different URLs

Mobile web personalization

Behavioral location based time based

Short, fast, simple

Customer journeys

Apps

-meeting a customer need

-utility value

-Device functionality

-Ease of use

Interactivity

Visibility in App stores

Leveraging handset functions (Evernote)

App development

7 step process

1. Justify
2. Build
3. Submit
4. Promote
5. Engage
6. Measure
7. Update

Module 8

App development, search and advertising

Justify

1. Customer benefit
2. Business benefit
3. Used handsets
4. Engagement plan
5. Promotion plan and benefit
6. Design, dev project must resource
7. App dev roadmap

Project Management

Think   Plan   Build

Customer feedback

Submit

Approval Time 3 weeks Apple 24 hours google

Promote

Banner ads

Email

Your own site

Engage

Location sensitive for foot traffic

Measure

Updates

Feedback

Different clues from tracking data

   Make new sites

   Thumb friendly

   Space around to move

   Mobile search extensions

Click-to-call site links click to download

Hyper local

   Metrics

Signed in Customers taking on customer journey to calculate adwords campaign

   Advertising

Brand/ Scale more responsiveness

   Module 8

   Advertising, SMS and Messaging

Mobile Campaign Process

Objectives, targeting, Budget trading, Creative comment materials, exporting, optimization evaluation

90% of SMSes are read within 3 minutes, Permission is essential, Raised awareness, Increased Participation

   Best Practices- SMS Campaigns

TU Ad

Press Ad

Board Ad

Bounce Back

Different Interactions

   Measurement

Delivery Rate

Open Rate

Opt-Out Rate

Click through Rate

Conversion Rate

   Data Integrated

URLs included in SMS

Who take cost

   Module 8

   Proximity Marketing and in coupons

Out of leave media location lazy marketing

Ibeacon Bluetooth (must be enabled) wake up app zones in starter

UFC (contactless payment) wear field communication

   Location Campaigns

   3rd party data and platforms

   Mobile coupons solve fraud

-create awareness in

-rebate redemption

-Social sharing (coupons)

   Module 8

   Strategy

   What is your business?

Mobile is owe channel

   How does mobile fit in?

KPIS- link back to budget

Keyword PPC matching organic search

Higher ranking with video

   Module 8

   Implementation and Laws

   Testing is fundamental

Key performance Indicators for mobile activity

Sources of traffic

Calculate where they are coming from

Keywords clicking on

Watch out for voice activation wearable technology

Live streaming periscope and market

Geo-location waze and swarm

Module 9

Introduction

Web analytics

"The collection, measurement and analysis of website data

Why

What is working?

Optimize a channel

Improve what is working

Justify and encourage investments to calculate value

Uses US customers

-Who uses analytics

-window into performance at any level

Can teach full user journey

Business goal – site analytics

Search pages   KPI Purchase product

Micro vs Macro Conversions

Platform campaign google analytics

Module 9

Google analytics

Access Levels

Manage users

Edit

Collaborate

Read and analyze

Setup account

Google.com/ analytics

Cant change time zone

Spend majority of time in reporting

Module 9

Audiences

Google analytics

Demographics reports – which is best for you

SEO – where are they coming from

Behavior

Returning visitors when they finally convert

Technology

Technology used to each site

Mobile

-Whats your mobile/ Desktop?

-tablet split?

-what type of device?

-Inform and shape future site development

-Inform and future advertising campaigns

Module 9

Acquisitions

Key section of different channels

Referrals

- what other sites drive traffic
- How does that traffic engage with my site?
- How do I go about getting more traffic from these sites?

Form permanent link?

Remarketing report

See how lists perform against analytics metrics (measure)

Social

What are my top social referrals

Search Engine Optimization

Evaluate your sites performance on search engines

Module 9

Behaviour

Designed to help improve the content of your site

Total # of views

Unique views

What pages are users most likely to exit the site from?

Understand your pages performance

Site search report

Are they satisfied with the results they get?

Events

Don't require an additional site link to load.

URL Builder Behavior

CA Tool (config)

Category/ action/ label

Module 9

Conversions

- Sections of analytics designed to help you Improve the performance of your website against your Key Performance Indicators

Goals

- Inquiry form completion
- Brochure request
- Goals should be relevant to the view they are created In.

View setting

Pre defined template

Use custom creating goals pages per session

More or less than page views

Goal tunnels

- Path to action
- Where are the biggest drop-offs
- Never use the homepage as Step 1

In the tunnel

Ecommerce

What are my top performance products?

Which products convert the best?

- Returns
- Which products are best for repeat purchases

Module 9

Attribution

The process of assigning a value to

each channel that played a role in a conversion.

Top conversions path report

- Top ten paths users took

As sited Conversions

See how channels played a role in conversations that other channels received credit for.

Model Comparison

- Time decay
- Last click – most widely used
- First click assigns full value
- Assigns value to each channel Linear – position based

Module 9

Customization, KPIs and case study

Making data unique to reporting data making sense for the business

Advanced Segments

- Compare paid search to all data
- Those who convert to those who don't.
- Create custom segments.

Range of conditions you can apply

Views

- Create new views through Admin tab
- Can have up to 25 views within a property

Filters

Add Filter to view for PPC traffic

- Default profile untouched
- Do not Apply filters
- Create multiple views to apply filters
- Always have unfiltered view
- Have a mixture
- Different filters for different products
- Focus on what's important to your business

Annotations

Allow you to record important events that could have an impact on your site

- Gives a clearer picture when analyzing the data historically.

Iteration

Defining and optimizing towards your KPIs

Module 9

Laws and Guidelines

- Onnice is on the business to obey the rules
- Notify when cookies in use
- Read through google analytics rules and regulations under terms and conditions.
- Work with senior management

Module 10

Introduction

Strategy and Planning Process

Effective strategy and planning is an iterative process involving goals, setup, manage and analyze.

- Structure campaign planning implications
- Budget
- Calendar organic with no end, 2014
- Personnel

Who is going to be on your team.

- Initiate – start with a customer
- Iterate continually trying things offline channels

Integrate traditional mix with the new.

"start with a customer and work backwards"

Google

- Keyword search tool

It's Funny

YOU SHOULD SAY THAT

JOAN MARJORY SILVERTHORN

DEDICATED TO

MY FAMILY AND FRIENDS, PAST AND PRESENT, IN THE U.K. AND CANADA—ALL OF WHOSE LOVING INFLUENCE AND HUMOUR CONTRIBUTED TO THIS BOOK: MY DEAREST HUBBY GLYN, AND DEAR "JOCK" WHO INTRODUCED US—OUR FINE CHILDREN JOHN AND ANNETTE AND THEIR FAMILIES. MY DEAR BROTHER PETE AND HIS FAMILY, MY KIND YOUNGER BROTHER JOHN AND HIS FINE WIFE VERA AND THEIR FAMILY, MY LOVELY SISTER-IN-LAW "RONNIE" AND DEAR HUBBY RAY, ALL THE CUTHBERT FAMILY—ESPECIALLY "AUNTIE GAG" AND MY BELOVED MOTHER "MARJIE": MRS. CATHERINE MARJORIE FRAZER WILLIAMS (NÉE CUTHBERT)

—A VERY KIND, SWEET, STRONG & FUNNY LADY.

POEM TO HER, FROM ME:
THEY SAY: "YOU *SHOULD* DO THIS
AND YOU
SHOULD DO THAT,
AND YOU
SHOULDN'T BE DOING THE OTHER."
BUT IF YOU WANT
TO KNOW HOW TO LIVE,
JUST LOOK AT MY BEAUTIFUL MOTHER.

—x—

A SPECIAL "THANKYOU" IS DUE TO MY DEAR GRANDSON, MATTHEW POPE, WHO ARRANGED AND FINANCED THE PRODUCTION OF THIS BOOK FOR ME, AND TO THE VERY HELPFUL PUBLISHERS

JOANZONE LITTLE COLLECTION
OF
SAGE SAYINGS & SILLY STORIES
PROFOUND & PERKY POEMS
COOL AND COMICAL COMMENTS
AND RIDICULOUS REMARKS
THANKS AND FAREWELL

PREFACE

"HERE I AM, SO THERE YOU ARE"
A POTTED (VERY) FAMILY STORY.

PREFACE

"HERE I AM, SO THERE YOU ARE."
—A POTTED (VERY) FAMILY STORY.

"I was born in very sorry circumstances—
Both my parents were very sorry—"
(JOKE) (I HOPE)

Actually, I was born in Newfoundland, now part of Canada. My
father, an Airship Pilot, was sent there to set up a Flying Station
in Botwood, but the weather was too bad for it to be practical. Whilst
there he was offered a job with the Hawkes Bay Trading Company,
so after his return to the U.K and the slowdown of Airship Flying, he
decided to take it. After a while my mother & brother joined him in
the "wilds". They lived in a log cabin and my mother learned to drive a
sleigh pulled by a dog team. (At one time, so the story goes, my brother,

then about 4, & bundled up in furs, rolled off the sledge as they were crossing a frozen lake, & a wide return sweep had to be made over the then cracking ice, to retrieve him.) I was born shortly afterwards & we moved to St. Johns, the capital. My earliest memory is of travelling to England in a creaky old boat, at the tender age of 2. (I also remember being a little pest, & wanting my dolls pram first up on deck & then below stairs, & also clambering onto the long seat all around the deck to "watch the waves," and nearly falling overboard. Poor Mother! She had a beautiful voice and used to sing to the Troops in WW1. She often sang songs from the Wild West to us—notably "Ragtime Cowboy Joe".

On returning to the U.K. my father renewed his Airship career for a while, having flown the first Airship from Italy to England. I clearly remember the ill-fated R101 flying over London, on its maiden trip to India, but it sadly crashed near Paris. Luckily my father was not among the crew. He then gave up flying as the Airship business was temporarily halted & went to work at de Havillands (in Edgware, North London, where we then lived.) as also did my brother, & later myself, as a wartime draughtswoman. (I worked in the "Prop.Test" Drawing Office on the Constant Speed Unit, fitted to propellers to allow the planes to fly higher & be more maneuverable.) During this time I met and married my husband, who was still in the RAF after nearly 9 years, & when his tour ended in 1946 he joined the Control Commission-(set up by the British Foreign Office, & made up of mostly ex-service personnel) & was sent to Germany as part of a team supervising the return of the airfields in Germany from their wartime footing to their new civilian government. I was later able to join him there & we lived firstly in Dusseldorf & then Hamburg. Whilst in Dusseldorf our son was born (In British Military Hospital No.22 in Wuppertal I remember!)

We returned to the U.K. after about 3 years in 1950, having made many good friends—British, German and International. In particular our Brit. Friends to this day, the Davies family (remembering dear Eddie and Ruth) and the Coward family (remembering dear John, "Ginh"), the MacDonald family, (remembering dear Molly) and of course the Nuthalls!

On our return from Germany we settled in the Hertfordshire village of Abbots Langley, England, where we spent many happy years, my husband having also taken a job at de Havillands, (then "Rolls-Royce") in Watford. Sadly though, & for no known reason, he developed Spondilitis of the spine, & after a few years died of leukemia, unfortunately brought on by the deep X-ray treatment used to cure it. (We were told at the time it was a risk, but he was in such pain he wanted to try it.) Throughout his illness he showed great courage and fortitude, as did our children. Towards the end, the stated in bed at weekends in order to gather strength enough to go to his job again every Monday morning, where he worked with his colleague Alex and their team to maintain the overhaul and repair of the Queen's Flight Helicopter engines, regularly having to report progress to the "Gentlemen from the Air Ministry".

He still showed consideration for others, overcoming his own pain and discomfort, and kept his sense of humour and proportion (which he passed on to his children!). He called his regular trips to "Barts" hospital (in London), for a complete change of blood via transformation, his "Top-Ups" and was very appreciative of the first-class attention and treatment he was given—as indeed we all were—a wonderful man—still deeply missed.

Our son John carried on with the apprenticeship his Dad had set up for him at Rolls-Royce, and saw it thro' the required 5 years which helped him forge an excellent career later on. Our daughter Annette took a commercial course & got herself a very good job in London. During his Apprenticeship years John also set up a private business in our garage at home, repairing and spraying cars, notably Minis (See poem "The Minis of Abbots"}and Triumph Heralds.

Later, John & his family emigrated to Canada, where he worked for Canadian Pacific Trail and Annette and I followed. She married & had 3 children there, & her brother returned with his wife & daughter Emma to the UK and was offered a good job with Minolta, U.K. later becoming their Business Development Manager. Having lived & worked in Calgary myself for 15 years (where the temperature "HIGH" was often 26° *below* in the winter!) I now go back & forth 6-monthly to Milton Keynes in the U.K., the home of the "Brit Bunch"(John and Charlotte, Emma and Leigh, Amy and Fiona) & Mission, near Vancouver B.C.—to visit the "Canajun Guys" (Annette and Matt, Robin and Cara, and John) and also keep my various pensions afloat.

I now rest my case...

P.S. How I came to be called "JOANZ"

Whilst in Calgary I worked as a draftsperson in an office lead by a charming Spanish Chief Draftsman (an ex-fighter pilot), I used to sign my drawings JOan S. (for Silverthorn) which he mistook for Joans, & would often call (politely) "JOANZ, would you please come here for a moment to discuss the work? Thank you so much."

ALTHOUGH I have spent 14 years as a psychotherapist dealing with emotional problems, there is a special group of helpless people I've been unable to counsel effectively. No television documentaries examine their curious ability to cope with everyday life; few magazine articles dissect their robust mental health. Many members of the group are even happily married. Who are these forgotten people? They are the well adjusted—and they have to be the most lonely inhabitants of one of the most neurotic societies in the history of the world. They are out of step. They just do not belong.

Yet this stable multitude need not despair. There is hope. With effort and a little perseverance, problems can be manufactured, guilt can be conveniently induced and neuroses nurtured. These unhappy extroverts have found a champion at last. All they really need to repair the psychic damage is a reliable guide to help them complicate their existence. This is a void I hope to fill. The following Ten Principles of Problem Production, earnestly applied, can make the lives of such misguided people truly and satisfyingly miserable.

Snowballing. This is a basic principle. If you face up to problems when they first appear, they tend to vanish. Don't make this fatal mistake. Let little problems get a firm foothold. Let them *snowball*.

When the income tax deadline looms, for instance, wait for a more convenient time before gathering the materials necessary for filing the forms. Avoid the temptation of putting records in a convenient place, thus assuring panic as income tax time comes closer and closer.

Expert snowballers follow a simple rule: "When it is past time to do something about a problem—wait a little longer." In marriage, for example, refuse to express feelings of irritation or anger for months, even years. This will build up enough pressure to blow your relationship apart.

The Reverse Beasley. This technique is named after my friend, Rod Beasley, who stubbornly refuses to internalize his problems. As a result, he is a hopeless failure at problem production and misses many opportunities to lose his composure. I was riding in a car with Beasley one day when he drew up to a four-way stop sign. He had barely paused when the man in the car behind us began blowing his horn. "That fellow is upset," I said.

Looking both ways as we slowly moved forward, Beasley answered: "That's *his* problem. My problem is to make sure this intersection is safe before proceeding. Horn-honking doesn't bother me."

Beasley simply refuses to assume those problems that belong to other people. By reversing his attitude, however, we formulate one of the cleverest problem-producing techniques. If you pay strict attention, you will succeed in lowering your self-esteem to a satisfactory level. Suppose someone doesn't like you. Assume the fault is yours, that there's something wrong with you. You'll soon be worrying yourself sick just trying to figure out what is is. Learn to say, "That is *my* problem." Blame yourself!

Negative Focus. Grow accustomed to looking on the dark side. Remember the times when you were treated unfairly or someone spoke unkindly to you. Say to yourself, I am *always* misunderstood and mistreated by everyone. Repeat this over and over as you sit in a dimly lit room listening to sad music. Beware the intrusion of happy thoughts. If you *should* think of something good about yourself, quickly remember a corresponding weakness. Focus on it! You can generate anything from anxiety to depression by the skillful use of negative thinking.

The I-Told-Me-So Syndrome. Also known as the Self-Fulfilling Prophecy, this technique is vital to sustaining problems. The idea is that if you *expect* bad things, they are much more likely to occur. If you are going to a party, predict you will not have a good time. Stand alone, away from the action. Later, bemoan the fact that no one would have anything to do with you.

The Impossible Dream. If you want to be frustrated, set your goals beyond reach. I once counseled a woman who was taking two college courses, learning to play the piano, caring for three children and looking after two sick relatives—all in addition to her regular job. She would not, she added, be satisfied with anything less than A's in her courses. Now *there* is an expert. No amateur could devise such an ego-breaking schedule. She is assured of suffering a high degree of frustration for years.

Ambiguous Goals. This principle can be stated as follows: Commitment to a lot of things is less than commitment to one thing and will always leave you uncertain about your accomplishments. Specificity is the hallmark of people who are solving their problems. Ambiguity is for the skilled problem-producer. Anyone who is sincere can blur his goals.

One way is to have contradictory aims. For example, if you want to be a really devoted housewife, then add to that goal one of developing a full-time career at the same time, out of town if possible. Another is never to finish what you start and so guarantee failure. This is especially good for college students. Begin in premed school, but tell yourself it is too hard. Switch to law, then to psychology, to business, to education, to engineering. An efficient goal-blurring expert can remain in school for 10 to 15 years without graduating.

The Fool's Golden Rule. Simply stated this rule says: Never give a damn about others. As a result, they will stop caring about you. This virtually guarantees aloneness and may evolve into severe loneliness.

The key to application of the rule is self-dislike. Say to yourself, "I'm no good. I have no value." Once you have lowered your self-esteem, it follows that other people are equally shallow. Treat them accordingly. Rejection is guaranteed.

Barrier Building. If you wake up one morning and discover that growth has occurred in your relationships with your wife and children, don't panic. Several general principles, consistently applied, will soon repair your crumbling barriers to understanding.

First, never compliment. Indeed, avoid any encouraging remarks—the truly troubled home is one where "never is heard an encouraging word." Next, step up criticism. Nag, complain, fuss. Finally, wield your financial clout. Tell your children, "As long as you drive *my* car, eat *my* food and live under *my* roof, you'll do as I say." Soon you will see their resentment build into a satisfying generation gap. With persistence and luck, they may someday blossom into full-blown rebels, and you'll have the problem you've worked so hard to construct.

Greener Grassing. No matter what you are doing, tell yourself it would be better to do something else. No matter whom you are married to, tell yourself that somewhere out there is a more compatible mate. Greener grassing can make your job *and* your marriage sheer hell.

Martyrdom. You can easily become a Joan or a John of Arc, if you put your mind to it. Mothers can overburden themselves with everyday household chores, then say to themselves, "No one really cares about me. As far as my family is concerned, I'm just a slave." Fathers can use the same approach: "I work my fingers to the bone, and no one gives a damn. Everyone uses me."

Burning yourself at the stake is not only helpful in generating feelings of self-disgust. It also dismays the people around you who quickly reject you.

The Ten Principles of Problem Production are negative. But they illustrate the control we have over our lives. They suggest that we not only can, but do, create problems—even illnesses—of our own accord. If you have recognized any of the principles, I hope you have been able to say, "Hey, that's what *I* do. I'm going to stop it, now!"

You will not always be privileged to do what you enjoy in life, but you have the power to enjoy most of what you do. You can produce problems—or overcome them. The choice is yours.

And don't forget to **PLAN AHEAD**

when i am
an old woman

I shall wear purple
With a red hat which doesn't go, and doesn't suit me.
And I shall spend my pension on brandy and summer gloves
And satin sandals, and say we've no money for butter.
I shall sit down on the pavement when I'm tired
And gobble up samples in shops and press alarm bells
And run my stick along the public railings
And make up for the sobriety of my youth.
I shall go out in my slippers in the rain
And pick the flowers in other people's gardens
And learn to spit.

You can wear terrible shirts and grow more fat
And eat three pounds of sausages at a go
Or only bread and a pickle for a week
And hoard pens and pencils and beermats and things in boxes.
But now we must have clothes that keep us dry
And pay our rent and not swear in the street
And set a good example for the children.
We will have friends to dinner and read the papers.
But maybe I ought to practise a little now?
So people who know me are not too shocked and surprised
When suddenly I am old and start to wear purple.

From Warning—by Jenny Joseph — Written Out by—Elizabeth Lucas

Daily Mail, Saturday, July 16, 2005

The three questions that show if you are up to the job

By **Stephanie Condron**

IMPRESSING prospective employers at a job interview could soon boil down to answering three questions correctly.

A brief IQ test is said to identify the cleverest candidates within minutes.

The Cognitive Reflection Test, which originated in the U.S., works on the premise that those of higher intelligence are more patient when trying to solve puzzles.

In one of the questions, candidates are asked: 'A bat and ball costs £1.10. The bat costs £1 more than the ball. How many pence does the ball cost?'

Those who reply '10p' tend to come up with the answer quickly – but incorrectly.

The smarter candidates, however, will still be pondering the puzzle.

If they come up with 5p - the correct answer – they are one step closer to getting the job.

'Anyone who reflects upon it for even a moment would recognise that the difference between £1 and 10p is only 90p, not £1 as the problem stipulates,' explained the test's designer, Professor Shane Frederick of the MIT Sloan School of Management in Massachusetts.

'In this case, catching that error is tantamount to solving the problem, since nearly everyone who does not respond "10p" does in fact give the correct response: "5p".'

Almost 3,500 students at 35 colleges took p.   study

to design the CRT test. But the test need not rely on the same three questions to work.

Psychologists have known for some time that those with patience tend to be more intelligent.

As predicted, those with the highest scores in the test tended to ponder longer when trying to answer the questions. Fewer than one in five (17 per cent) answered all three correctly. A third got all

three wrong. There was also a big difference between sexes.

Men were much better at the test than women, making up two thirds of those with the highest scores. Two thirds of those scoring lowest were female.

American IQ and personality tests are increasingly being used by British employers for recruitment. But they are often expensive and can take hours to complete.

HOW WOULD YOU FARE?

1 A bat and ball cost £1.10 in total. The bat costs £1 more than the ball. How many pence does the ball cost?

2 If it takes five machines, five minutes to make five widgets, how many minutes would it take 100 machines to make 100 widgets?

3 In a lake there is a patch of lily pads. Every day the patch doubles in size. If it takes 48 days for the patch to cover the entire lake, how many days would it take for the patch to cover half the lake?

Answers – 1: 5p. 2: five minutes 3: 47 days

Dedicated to dear Charlotte, Amy and Fiona

JOANZ "POMES"

Hang on fast
To Joy & Beauty—
Never let them go.
Only then
You'll find a balance
In this world of woe.

Full of troubles,
Work & duty,
Seems it never ends—
But you'll still find love & fun,
With family & friends

Hang on fast
To things of beauty—
Never let them die,
Then in times
Of trial & trouble,
They will get you by.

—x—

It takes you all your life
To learn how to live the life
It takes you all your life
To learn how to live!

—x—

JUST A MOMENT

Stop striving for Perfection
And you will quickly find
A change in the direction
For your tortured troubled mind
There's simply "No such Animal"
In all the world you see,
So do your best, then take a rest
And simply "LET IT BE".

JOANZ "POMES"

Dedicated to our fine son John and his pals: Cris B., Jim C., Gerry A., Peter M., "Spud" (Nigel) T., Ian B., Terry G., Steve W., Ian M., Martin G., Dick S., Dave A., Fred D., and all involved. (Hope I haven't missed any. It was 44 years ago...)

At one point we had more than a dozen pals all chatting and joking by the garage door, and I had to reluctantly ask a few to leave (temporarily) saying the "regulars" could stay, in consideration for our long suffering (tho' always kind and understanding) neighbours.

P.S. Triumph Heralds were beautifully restored too, as were many other cards and trucks, but I ran out of rhyme!

THE MINIS OF ABBOTS

Oh I still miss
The Minis of Abbots,
(In 1965).
And all the lads
Who flew around
So happy & alive.
They were decent lads,
And clever lads,
Who taught themselves to fix
Their bikes & cars
(And Mum's & Dad's)
And soon learned all the tricks
Of *rubbing down* & *filling priming*
Then *spraying* (blue, yellow or red)
They gave themselves apprenticeships
Which stood them in good stead.
And they turned out
The finest jobs
That you have ever seen—
Beautiful MINS with Vinyl roofs
Some *British Racing Green*.
A Club was formed
At 34
(Though quite unconsciously)
A dozen often gathered there
To share their jokes & tea.
So witty they were,
But apparently,
Not known by them (nor I)
The cellulose paint

With which they worked
Was a spray that made them High!
Tho' it was fun
Something must be done
To stop it getting thro'
This was Agreed
When someone Pee'd
In Royal Pacific Blue!
T'was the same back then,
-No-one listened when
It's what a *Parent* asks—
But finally
They came to see
T'was time for wearing MASKS!

So—life moves on—
And strange to say,
Although the time has flown,
Now all their wives
And children too
Have MINIS of their own.

"MULL OF KINTYRE"

MULL OF KINTYRE,
O, MULL OF KINTYRE,
WHAT A BEAUTIFUL SOUNDING NAME—
CONJURING DREAMS
OF BEAUTY AND MYSTERY,
FAR TOO WILD TO TAME.
BUT NOW, WITH THE LOSS
OF NINE FINE LIVES
IN A TERRIBLE BALL OF FIRE,
YOU NEVER WILL SOUND
THE SAME AGAIN,
O, TREACHEROUS MULL OF KINTYRE.

Joan Silverthorn

Dedicated to Sarah, Colin, and Luke and family (remembering dear Irene)

JOANZ PERKY "POMES"

Have you heard the one about
My Grannie & her Runabout?
She thought it was a TR4,
And travelled motorways galore.
A Lotus tried, but couldn't match her—
Even cop-cars couldn't catch her—
Till suddenly disaster struck,
She was o'ertaken by a truck
Which pulled ahead & blocked her way.
At which point she was heard to say:
"I'll get the better of 'em yet—
I'll get it fitted with a jet."
Then next they saw her over Harrow,
Whizzing past a lone "Red Arrow"—
(No-one could call my Gran a whimp)
But then she hit a Branson Blimp—
Together they came drifting down,
Somewhere over London Town.
And so her fun came to an end.
But let this be a warning, friend—
If your Gran gets a Runabout,
Be sure you're there when she goes OUT!

—x—

"SAME OLD..."

In this world
of new Ideas,
And Marvelous Inventions,
The same old Road to Hell
Will still
Be paved with Good Intentions.

—x—

Some women only seem
Flippant & chattery—
Interested only
In men & their flattery,
Prattling along
Till they need a new battery—
Oh! What a LOT, women are!

Fooling around
When they're s'posed to be serious,
Carrying on
Till they're all quite delirious—
To the mere male
They're completely mysterious.
Oh! Such a LOT, women are!

Yet when her man
Has been out on a Bender,
His wife can be
Quite understanding & tender—
Making him ready
To DIE to defend her—

Oh! What a LOT we all are!

—x—

There was an old lady from Streatham
Who choked on her false teeth, & ate 'em—
Her doctor said "Look—
I've got this wee hook
Which I'll drop down your throat
And we'll get 'em!"

—x—

How very sad, it seems to me,
That people have to "WIN"-
Just to be RIGHT
Is their delight
And to be WRONG, a SIN!
The narrow mind
And shallow heart
Displayed for all to see,
Will send a message, others find,
Of Insecurity.
How sad it is, not to allow
Their souls to travel free,
And share the flow of all ideas,
Before they DISAGREE.

—x—

She was the kind of person
Who only asked for your opinion
So that she could disagree with it

—x—

He was the kind of person
Who couldn't wait to hear
What he was going to say next.

—x—

Four of the most beautiful words
In the English Language:
"Sorry, I was wrong."

—x—

Dedicated to Ernest Errington Reid, a writer and poet himself, who, with his lovely wife, Josephine, always encouraged me in this precarious adventure!

"CHOICE"

IF I SO CHOOSE,
I CAN EMERGE
FROM ALL THE SCARS UNSCATHED—
CAST OFF EACH SHAFT
THAT FATE IMPARTS
AS A BABY WHEN IT'S BATHED.

IF I SO CHOOSE
I'LL SOFTLY TREAD,
MY CITADEL INTACT,
IN A HOMESPUN WEB OF LIGHT
THRO' DARK REALITY'S ATTACK.

BUT WHICH IS REAL?
THE DARK OR LIGHT?
THE CHOICE IS MINE.

—x—

THE BEST THING YOU
CAN EVER DO
IS LOVE YOURSELF
AND OTHERS TOO.

Dedicated to dear friend Jim Weir and his family (remembering dear Joan and "Jock")

COMPUTER BLUES

Many a mouse
Has been chucked thro' the house,
Many a Monitor cursed,
Many a screen
Has heard language obscene,
And been threatened with deeds
Of the worst.
Many a sane & intelligent man
Has turned into someone quite rude;
And torn out his hair
In an act of despair,
And threatened reprisals quite lewd.
"To heck with the mates
Of the worthy Bill Gates—
Can't they do better than this?
If not, then I'm sorry,
I'm not going to worry—
I'm just going to blow them a kiss…
I'd felt quite depraved,
When the text that I'd saved
Was nowhere at all to be seen—
But what's this appearing?
The stuff I'd been fearing
Was lost, is now here on the screen!
'Cos all of a sudden,
I pressed the right button
And up came the work that I'd lost!
So, suddenly—MAGIC! Things don't seem so TRAGIC

I've even stopped counting the cost
Of the hours I've spent
Over keyboard well bent,
Trying my best to be calm.
And stop myself yelling,
Whilst anger was swelling
A risk of inflicting some harm.
Now—should I get tough,
And handle it rough,
Or be gentle & kind in my dealings?
Perhaps after all,
I made it feel small,
And hurt its poor Internet feelings…
But, what if it gets
All contrary again,
Even before I get started?
I know, even so, I just can't let it go…
OH! COMPUTERS ARENT FOR THE FAINT-HEARTED!

—x—

One of the worst moments
For an Atheist
Is when he is truly thankful,
But has nobody to thank.

—x—   ANON

It's easy enough to be cheerful, When life rolls along
like a song— But the man worth his while
Is the one who can smile
When everything goes DEAD WRONG!

—x—   ANON

Life is mostly froth & bubble- Two things stand like stone.
Kindness in another's trouble, Courage in your own.

—x—   *ANON*

SILENT & LISTEN are spelt with
The same letters.

—x—

When someone asks me *Whatever* I do with my
time, Now that I'm old & "retired",
My answer is
"How long have you got...?"

—x—

JOANZ "POMES"

To Mike, with love
Life all seems full,
Of Jiggery Pokery—
Sometimes it feels like
A regular Jokery—
Almost as if someone's
Making a Mockery—
Oh, what a crazy
old Life

—x—

My Wish
I'd like to banish
All your fears,
And cancel irritation-
I'd like to fill
Your heart with cheer
And bring your soul elation!

—x—

Draftmen's Remarks:—
(on backs of boards)

"Everybody is entitled to
my opinion"

WORK!—but I guess it
gives you something to
do while you're here.

Do you come here often?

All most people really
want is to be left alone
to live out their lives
in a state of quiet desperation...

Draffy on messing up his drawing
"Oh, *LORD*"
Entire Office: "YES...?"

"I SAW, a bumper sticker the other day that made me feel so proud. It said: "Love America! Think America! Keep America Strong!" Only one problem: it was on the back of a Toyota!—*Mason Seglin, Chicago, Illinois*

QUESTION Which is the best way for me to ensure my watch is set accurately?

Dedicated to the Querido Family

FURTHER to the earlier answer, Cape Town, in South Africa, used to have a unique method of timekeeping—a noon-day gun would be fired from the foot of Table Mountain.

Some time ago I watched the procedure. The field gun was a very fine item of artillery, and both gunners were friendly and informative. But, seeing that they had no radio, I asked how they knew it was noon.

They pointed to a telescope directed at a clock outside a jeweller's shop in the town, which they declared was the finest clock in the Cape.

As noon approached, one of the men observed the clock, and when the hands indicated high noon he shouted 'Fire!' and the gun boomed out over the city.

Later in the day I found myself outside the jeweller's, admiring the clock. The owner joined me and explained that it had been imported from Amsterdam in the last century, and was the finest time-keeper in all South Africa.

I asked him if he checked it with radio signals. 'No need,' he said. 'Every day they fire a noon-day gun on the mountain.'

John Matthews,
Llanllweh, Carmarthan,
Wales, U.K.

MIKE WAGGONER

A visitor to a factory that manufactures computers inquired about what went on behind a door marked "Super-Stars." "Oh," said the guide, "That's a special department where they are working on very advanced models. We have one that is practically human."

"You mean," asked the visitor, "that it will think?"

"Well, not quite," replied the guide, but it will blame its mistakes on other computers."

"You always lend me these old things! Why don't you splurge on an electric trimmer?"

"Can you fix them by Saturday? I'm in the finals."

"Have you finished with the financial section?"

"WHY?"—

Does anyone have the answers?

Why does the sun lighten our hair, but darkens our skin?

Why can't women put on mascara with their mouth closed?

Why don't you ever see the headline "Psychic Wins Lottery"?

Why is "abbreviated" such a long word?

Why is it that doctors call what they do "practice"?

Why is it that to stop Windows, you have to click on "Start"?

Why is lemon juice made with artificial flavour and dish washing liquid made with real lemons?

Why is the man who invests all your money called a broker?

Why is the time of day with the slowest traffic called rush hour?

Why isn't there mouse-flavoured cat food?

When dog food is new and improved tasting, who tests it?

Why didn't Noah swat those two mosquitoes?

Why do they sterilise the needle for lethal injections?

Why don't sheep shrink when it rains?

Why is there only one Monopolies Commission?

PHIL KEMPTON

HERMAN

"Have you finished with
the financial section?"

Daily Mail, Saturday, July 16, 2005

A truck driver pulled into a cafe at a highway truck stop for a stay-awake cup of coffee. Shortly, a rough and tough motorcycle gang of eight roared up, parked and swaggered inside. The leader of the gang looked around and decided to show his power. He walked over and stuck his cigar into the trucker's coffee. They fixed each other with glares, but nothing happened. The truck driver paid his check and drove off.

"Not much of a man, that trucker," said the cycle boss.

"Not much of a truck driver either," said the waitress. "Just as he was leaving, he ran over eight motorcycles."

Meanwhile, in the Restaurant across the street...

In an ancient Monastery in a faraway place a new monk arrived to join his brothers in copying books and scrolls in the monastery's scriptorium. He was assigned as a authenticator on copies of books that had already been copied by hand.

One day he asked Father Florian "Does not the copying by hand of other copies allow for chances of error? How do we know we are not copying the mistakes of someone else? Are they ever checked against the original?"

Fr. Florian was set back a bit by the obvious logical observation of this youthful monk. "A very good point, my son. I will take one of the latest books down to the vault and compare it against the original." Fr. Florian went down to the secured vault and began his verification.

After a day had passed, the monks began to worry and went down looking for the old priest. They were sure something must have happened. As they approached the vault, they heard sobbing and crying. When they opened the door, they found Fr. Florian sobbing over the new copy and the original ancient book, both of which were opened before him on the table. It was obvious to all that the poor man had been crying his old heart out for a long time. "What is the problem Reverend Father?" asked one of the monks. "Oh my Lord," sobbed the priest, "the word is *CELEBRATE*"...

ANON

'We apologise to passengers for the severe delays.
Rest assured our engineers are working
flat out to trace the computer fault...'

Living off campus? You know your apartment is small when...

...flies must file a flight plan.

...you can answer the telephone from the bed, the kitchen table, the sink or the shower.

...your wall-to-wall carpet is a welcome mat.

...Rice Krispies echo.

...you can have breakfast in bed without getting up to fix it.

...one is company, and two is a crowd.—S. Rickly Christian in *Campus Life*

SAD TALE

Little Bobby drank,
But now he'll
Drink no more-
'Cos what he thought
Was H20
Was H2S04...

—x—

Dedicated to dear Emma and Leigh

SELF IMPROVEMENT WORKSHOPS

Creative Suffering
Overcoming Peace of Mind
You and Your Birthmark
Guilt Without Sex
The Primal Shrug
Ego Gratification Through Violence
Holding With Post Self-Realization Depression
Whine You Way to Alienation
Be Obnoxious Through Assertiveness Training
How to Overcome Self-Doubt Through Pretense and Ostentation

BUSINESS AND CAREER WORKSHOPS

Money Can Make You Rich
I Made $100 in Real Estate
Talking Good: How You Can Improve Speech and
Get a Better Job Career Opportunities in Iran
How to Profit From Your Own Body
Underachievers Guide to Very Small Business
Opportunities Filler Phrases for Thesis Writers
Tax Shelters for the Indigent
Looter's Guide to American Cities

HOME ECONOMICS WORKSHOPS

How You Can Convert Your Family Room Into a Garage
How to Cultivate Viruses in Your Refrigerator
Burglar-proof Your Home with a Concrete Bunker
Basic Kitchen Taxidermy
Sinus Drainage at Home
101 Uses for Your Vacuum Cleaner
Repair and Maintenance of your Virginity
How to Convert a Wheelchair into a Dune Buggy
What to do With Your Conversation Pit
Christianity and the Art of RV Maintenance

HEALTH AND FITNESS WORKSHOPS

Creative Tooth Decay
Exorcism and Acne
The Joys of Hypochondria
High Fiber Sex
Suicide and Your Health
Bio-feedback and How to Stop It
Skate your Way to Regularity
Understanding Nudity
Optional Body Functions
Tap Dance Your Way to Social Ridicule

CRAFTS WORKSHOPS

Self-Actualization Through Macrame
How to Draw Genitalia
Needlecraft & Junkies
Northern California Guide to Bad Taste
Cuticle Crafts
Mobiles & Collages With Fetishes
Gifts for the Senile
Margarine Carvings
Political Cartooning With Stained Glass

ANON

HOW WOULD YOU FARE?

1. A bat and ball cost £1.10 in total. The bat costs £1 more than the ball. How many pence does the ball cost?
2. If it takes five machines, five minutes to make five widgets, how many minutes would it take 100 machines to make 100 widgets?
3. In a lake there is a patch of lily pads. Every day the patch doubles in size. If it takes 48 days for the patch to cover the entire lake, how many days would it take for the patch to cover half the lake?

Answers—1: 5p; 2: five minutes; 3: 47 days

The three questions that show if you are up to the job

By Stephanie Condron

IMPRESSING prospective employers at a job interview could soon boil down to answering three questions correctly.

A brief IQ test is said to identify the cleverest candidates within minutes.

The Cognitive Reflection Test, which originated in the U.S., works on the premise that those of higher intelligence are more patient when trying to solve puzzles.

In one of the questions, candidates are asked: 'A bat and ball costs £1.10. The bat costs £1 more than the ball.

'How many pence does the ball cost?'

Those who reply '10p' tend to come up with the answer quickly—but incorrectly.

The smarter candidates, however, will still be pondering the puzzle.

If they come up with 5p—the correct answer—they are one step closer to getting the job.

'Anyone who reflects upon it for even a moment would recognize that the difference between £1 and 10p is only 90p, not £1 as the problem stipulates,' explained the test's designer, Professor Shane Frederick of the MIT Sloan School of Management in Massachusetts.

'In this case, catching that error is tantamount to solving the problem, since nearly everyone who does not respond "10p" does in fact give the correct response: "5p".'

Almost 3,500 students at 35 colleges took part in his study to design the CRT test. But the test need not rely on the same three questions to work.

Psychologists have known for some time that those with patience tend to be more intelligent.

As predicted, those with the highest scores in the test tended to ponder longer when trying to answer the questions. Fewer than one in five (17 per cent) answered all three correctly. A third got all three wrong. There was also a big difference between sexes.

Men were much better at the test than women, making up two thirds of those with the highest scores. Two thirds of those scoring lowest were female.

American IQ and personality tests are increasingly being used by British employers for recruitment. But they are often expensive and can take hours to complete.

JOANZ PERKY POMES—SAGE SAYINGS
JOANZ SAGE SAYINGS

You know you're in trouble when
You catch yourself harmonizing to
You're own Tinnitus

You know you're not old if you
Can still cut your own toenails
And what's more, remember doing it.

He was so tough, he ate
Brillo Pads for breakfast.

To ASSUME makes
An ASS out of
U & ME.

You don't get a second chance
To make a First Impression…

If something goes without saying,
It's probably better to let it.

Cynics' Corner:
Life is the wonderful, Sick Joke
That comes with Free Will

—x—

Come on in—my day's ruined anyway—

—x—

It's better to be alone, than to wish you were.

I'm the Secretary of
The Seriously Underwhelmed Society.

I never repeat gossip,
So listen very carefully.

Ever noticed that the people
Who tell you to *calm down* are the very
Ones who got you mad in the first place...?

It's never too late to have A Happy Childhood.

My mind is made up,
Don't confuse me with the facts.

TIPS ON CAT GROOMING

1. Thoroughly clean the toilet.
2. Add the required amount of shampoo to the toilet water and have both lids up.
3. Find the cat and soothe him while you carry him towards the bathroom.
4. In one smooth movement, put the cat in the toilet and close both lids. (You may need to stand on the lid so that he cannot escape.) The cat will self-agitate and make ample suds. Never mind the noises that come from your toilet, the cat is actually enjoying this. CAUTION: Do not get any part of your body too close to the edge, as his paws will be reaching out for anything they can find.
5. Flush the toilet three or four times. This provides a "Power Wash and Rinse", which I have found to be quite effective.
6. Have someone open the door to the outside and ensure that there are no people between the toile and the outside door.
7. Stand behind the toilet as far as you can, and quickly lift both lids.
8. The now clean cat will rocket out of the toilet, and run outside where he will dry himself.

Sincerely,
The Dog

TIMMIE'S SPECIAL

I'm just a CASUAL CAT I am,
Yerz, just a CASUAL CAT.
But I know *where it's at* I do,
Do I know *where it's at*!
Oh People come, & People go,
They fret & fume & fuss,
But I just go my casual way,
Content to be a PUSS.

BITZ ON BAX OF CARZ

"NOT SO CLOSE, I HARDLY KNOW YOU."

—x—

"AS A MATTER OF FACT I DO OWN THE ROAD."

—x—

"OF COURSE I'M ALLOWED TO USE ALL 3 LANES"

—x—

"DON'T OVERTAKE WITHOUT MY PERMISSION"

—x—

"PLEASE OVERTAKE, RUNNING IN"

—x—

"PLEASE OVERTAKE, WEARING OUT"

—x—

CALL FROM BEHIND,
TO THE GUY SITTING AT THE LIGHTS:
"THEY'RE NOT GOING TO GET ANY GREENER…"

—x—

SEATBELTS ARE NOT AS CONFINING
AS WHEELCHAIRS.

—x—

I'M NOT SO THUNK AS YOU DRINK I AM.

—x—

"It's a perfectly lousy club, but I can't seem to throw it away."
NATIONAL ENQUIRER

"Let's forget about the ball and find the course"

Dedicated to dear school pals (since 1936): Naomi Salter (Née Baker) and Joan Carter (Née Starmer) (Remembering dear Freddie and Dot and Yvonne) Also Pearl Preece (Née Benson) Old pal since 1940 (Remembering dear David) and all their families.

Original message
From: Coralee Vescarelli
Subject: Fwd: Church Ladies & Typewriters

Take a minute to read these… even if you've read them before. You know, "laughter is the best medicine".

CHURCH LADIES & TYPEWRITERS

Thank God for church ladies with typewriters. These sentences actually appeared in church bulletins or were announced in church services:

1. Bertha Belch, a missionary from Africa, will be speaking tonight at Calvary Methodist. Come hear Bertha Belch all the way from Africa.
2. Announcement in a church bulletin for a national PRAYER & FASTING Conference: "The cost for attending the Fasting & Prayer Conference includes meals."
3. This was too unkind to repeat.
4. Our youth basketball team is back in action Wednesday at 8 PM in the recreation hall. Come out and watch—DITTO—
5. "Ladies, don't forget the rummage sale. It's a chance to get rid of those things not worth keeping around the house. Don't forget your husbands.
6. The peacemaking meeting scheduled for today has been cancelled due to a conflict.
7. Remember in prayer the many who are sick of our community. Smile at someone who is hard to love. Say "Hell" to someone who doesn't care much about you.
8. Don't let worry kill you off—let the Church help.
9. Miss Charlene Mason sang "I will not pass this way again," giving obvious pleasure to the congregation.
10. For those of you who have children and don't know it, we have a nursery downstairs.
11. Next Thursday there will be tryouts for the choir. They need all the help they can get.
12. Barbara remains in the hospital and needs blood donors for more transfusions. She is also having trouble sleeping and requests tapes of Pastor Jack's sermons.

13. The Rector will preach his farewell message after which the choir will sing: "Break Forth Into Joy."
14. Irving Benson and Jessie Carter were married on October 24th in the church. So ends a friendship that began in their school days.
15. A bean supper will be held on Tuesday evening in the church hall. Music will follow.
16. At the evening service tonight, the sermon topic will be "What Is Hell?" Come early and listen to our choir practice.
17. Eight new choir robes are currently needed due to the addition of several new members and to the deterioration of some older ones.
18. Scouts are saving aluminum cans, bottles and other items to be recycled. Proceeds will be used to cripple children.
19. Please place your donation in the envelope along with the deceased person you want remembered.
20. Attend and you will hear an excellent speaker and heave a healthy lunch.
21. The church will host an evening of fine dining, superb entertainment and gracious hostility.
22. Potluck supper Sunday at 5:00 PM—prayer and medication to follow.
23. The ladies of the Church have cast off clothing of every kind. They may be seen in the basement on Friday afternoon.
24. This evening at 7 PM there will be a hymn sing in the park across from the Church. Bring a blanket and come prepared to sin.
25. Ladies Bible Study will be held Thursday morning at 10 AM. All ladies are invited to lunch in the Fellowship Hall after the B.S. is done.
26. The pastor would appreciate it if the ladies of the congregation would lend him their electric girdles for the pancake breakfast next Sunday.
27. Low Self Esteem Support Group will meet Thursday at 7 PM. Please use the back door.

28. The eighth-graders will be presenting Shakespeare's Hamlet in the Church basement Friday at 7 PM. The congregation is invited to attend this tragedy.
29. Weight Watchers will meet at 7 PM at the First Presbyterian Church. Please use large double door at the side entrance.

Cookbook

Indian Butter Chicken Serves 4
- 1 packet Indian Butter Chicken Spice Paste
- 3 tbsp melted butter
- 1 large onion, finely chopped
- ½ cup (110 mL) tomato puree or chopped tomatoes (fresh or canned)
- ½ cup (110 mL) water
- ½ cup (110 mL) double cream or yoghurt, reserve 1 tbsp to garnish
- 450 g (1 lb) deboned rabbit, tandoori or fresh chicken, cut into bite-sized pieces
- Fresh coriander as garnish (optional)

Poulet au beurre indien Donne 4 portions
- 1 sachet de pâte d'épices pour poulet au beurre indien
- 3 c. à table de beurre fondu
- 1 gros oignon, émincé
- ½ tasse (110 mL) de purée de tomate ou de tomates hachées (fraîches ou en boîte)
- ½ tasse (110 mL) d'eau
- ½ tasse (110 mL) de double crème ou de yogourt, réserver 1 c. à table pour garnir
- 450 g (1 lb) de poulet nu, de poulet tandoori ou de poulet frais, désossé et coupé en petits morceaux
- Coriandre fraîche en garniture (facultatif)

1. Heat butter in a non-stick saucepan on medium heat; add onion and stir-fry for 3 minutes.
   Faire chauffer le beurre à feu moyen dans une casserole antiadhésive, ajouter les oignons et faire sauter 3 minutes.

2. Stir in tomato puree, water, cream and Spice Paste.
   Incorporer la purée de tomate, l'eau, la crème et la pâte d'épices.

3. Add meat, simmer uncovered on low heat for 20 minutes or until it thickens. Garnish with cream or yoghurt. Serve hot.
   Ajouter la viande, mijoter à découvert à feu doux 20 minutes ou jusqu'à ce que la préparation épaississe. Garnir avec la crème ou le yogourt. Servir chaud.

Ingredients: Tomato paste (23%), soybean oil, onion, salt, sugar, ground coriander, red chillies, garlic, vinegar, ginger, herbs and spices, cayenne, pepper, acid regulator (citric acid).

Ingrédients: pâte de tomates (23%), huile de soja, sel, sucre, coriandre moulu, piments rouges, ail, vinaigre, gingembre, herbes et épices, cayenne, poivre, régulateur de l'acidité (acide citrique).

Manufactured for / Fabriqué pour:
Asian Home Gourmet (CPL) Pte Ltd
under licence from / sous licence de
Cerebos Pacific Ltd.
400 Orchard Road, #11-12,
Orchard Towers, Singapore 238875
Email / courriel: info@asianhomegourmet.com

Product of Thailand / Produit de Thaïlande

Nutrition Facts
Valeur nutritive
Per ¼ package (13 g)
par ¼ d'emballage (13 g)

Amount / Teneur		% Daily Value / % Valeur quotidienne
Calories / Calories 30		
Fat / Lipides 2 g		3 %
Saturated / saturés 0 g + Trans / trans 0 g		0 %
Cholesterol / Cholestérol 0 mg		
Sodium / Sodium 430 mg		18 %
Carbohydrate / Glucides 1 g		1 %
Fiber / Fibres 1 g		2 %
Sugars / Sucres 1 g		
Protein / Protéines 1 g		
Vitamin A / Vitamine A		0 %
Vitamin C / Vitamine C		0 %
Calcium / Calcium		0 %
Iron / Fer		0 %

Keep away from direct sunlight and store in cool dry place. Once opened, use immediately.
Conserver à l'abri du soleil, dans un endroit frais et sec. Utiliser immédiatement après l'ouverture.

Imported by / Importé par
Elco Fine Foods Inc.
Markham, Ontario, L3R 3W6
info@elcofinefoods.com

0 15205 72030 1

Honey-Balsamic Baked Chicken with Tomatoes, Mushrooms & Peppers

Serves four.
by Abigail Johnson Dodge from Fine Cooking Issue 38

While the chicken cooks to a deep brown color, the vegetables in the pan simmer into a delicious chunky sauce to serve with the chicken.

---

1 chicken (3-1/2 to 4 lb.), cut into quarters

1 medium red bell pepper, cored, seeded, and cut into 1-inch pieces

1 medium yellow bell pepper, cored, seeded, and cut into 1-inch pieces

1/2 lb. mushrooms (button, cremini, or other), cleaned and cut into quarters

14-1/2-oz. can diced tomatoes, drained

3 Tbs. olive oil

2 Tbs. balsamic vinegar

1 Tbs. chopped fresh rosemary

1-1/2 tsp. coarse salt

Freshly ground black pepper

1-1/2 Tbs. honey

Heat the oven to 425°F. Rinse the chicken and pat it dry with paper towels. Cut away any excess fat and tuck the wings behind each breast.

In a large, shallow baking pan (the 10-1/2x15 1/2-inch Pyrex is ideal), toss the peppers, mushrooms, and tomatoes. Drizzle the oil and balsamic vinegar over the vegetables and sprinkle with the rosemary, 1/2 tsp. salt, and lots of freshly ground pepper. Toss until well coated. Dredge the chicken pieces, skin side down, in the vegetable mixture so that they get coated in the oil and vinegar and turn them over. Sprinkle with the remaining 1 tsp. salt and more pepper. Drizzle the skin with the honey. Bake until the chicken is well browned and cooked through, 50 to 60 minutes.

---

nutrition information (per serving):

Calories (kcal): 640; Fat (g): fat g 37; Fat Calories (kcal): 330; Saturated Fat (g): sat fat g 10; Protein (g): protein g 56; Monounsaturated Fat (g): 18; Carbohydrates (g): carbs g 23; Polyunsaturated Fat (g): 7; Sodium (mg): sodium mg 1010; Cholesterol (mg): cholesterol mg 210; Fiber (g): fiber g 4;

★ ★ ★ ★ ★ by Helen_W, 9/20/2015 This recipe is absolutely delicious and so easy! I used chicken thighs instead of a quartered chicken. I didn't have fresh mushrooms on hand so I substituted a medium yellow squash. And, I had mixed

Masoor Dhal

This spicy lentil dish, flavored with onion, garlic, and lemon juice, is high in nutrients as well as tasting delicious, so you can feel good about its benefits as well as enjoying its fantastic flavors.

4 tablespoons oil
6 cloves
6 cardamoms
1-inch piece of cinnamon stick
1 onion, chopped
1-inch piece of fresh ginger root, chopped
1 fresh green chile, finely chopped
1 garlic clove, chopped
½ teaspoon garam masala
1¼ cups lentils
4 tablespoons lemon juice
salt
2-3 dried chiles, to garnish (optional)

heat the oil in a pan, add the cloves, cardamoms, and cinnamon and fry until they start to swell.

add the onion and cook until translucent. Add the ginger, chile, garlic, and garam masala and cook for about 5 minutes.

add the lentils, stir thoroughly, and cook for 1 minute. Add salt to taste and enough water to come about 1½ inches above the level of the lentils. Bring to the boil, cover, and simmer for about 20 minutes, until really thick and tender.

sprinkle with the lemon juice, stir and serve immediately, garnished with dried chiles, if liked.

Serves 4
Preparation time: *20 minutes*
Cooking time: *25 minutes*

clip**board:** Lentils are full of nutrients...

YELLOW LENTIL SOUP

REVIEWS ( )   MAKE IT AGAIN

Editor's note: This recipe is adapted from Magda el-Mehdawy's book My Egyptian Grandmother's Kitchen. _Mehdawy also shared some helpful tips exclusively with Epicurious, which we've added at the bottom of the page. To read more about Mehdawy and Egyptian cuisine,   ._

Lentils are a very ancient food staple, and have been the basis of diets in the Middle East for millennia. To perk up the flavor of this soup, cooks often add a spritz of lemon juice to each serving at the last minute.

SAVE RECIPE   ADD TO MENU

COOK   REVIEWS (   )

INGREDIENTS

- 1 tablespoon ghee (clarified butter, see Tips, below)

- 2 rounds pita bread, each cut into 9 wedges

- 1 pound dried yellow lentils

- 1 medium tomato, quartered and seeded

- 1 medium potato, peeled and cut into 1 inch slices

- 1 medium carrot, peeled and cut into 1 inch slices

- 2 teaspoons salt

- 1 tablespoon corn oil

- 1 large onion, finely chopped

- 3 cups beef stock or canned beef broth

- 1 teaspoon ground cumin

- 1 tablespoon chopped fresh parsley

PREPARATION

In large skillet over medium heat, heat ghee. Working in batches of 6, sauté pita pieces until crisp, about 4 minutes per side. Drain on paper towels and set aside.

Very easy & very good! Thanks to all for their previous comments, as usual, that helped immensely!! Doubled the recipe (party in 2 days) - DID NOT blend, but did rice the extra carrots (no potatoes) fabulous color and flavor! Sauteed the onions, shallots, garlic, tomato paste with cumin and tumeric ... added that to the original pot which now had only the lentils and riced carrots. Squeezed a full lemon and wow ... what an aroma!! Will add cilantro vs the parsley, can't wait!!

It was some work, but my family and I really liked it; full flavor. I used olive oil instead of gee, and and vegetable broth.

A lot of work for a mediocre pay off. I strongly distrust these cooking times and the taste was bland to say the least. Other user reviews and tips were the only reason this recipe some-what worked. If--and that's a big IF--I do this recipe again, I'll definitely add a whole chipotle to the pot for some flavor.

RELATED
RECIPES

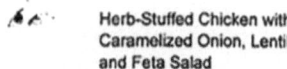
Herb-Stuffed Chicken with
Caramelized Onion, Lentil,
and Feta Salad

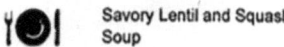
Savory Lentil and Squash
Soup

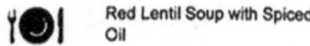
Red Lentil Soup with Spiced
Oil

Cashew Soup

Spicy Lamb and Lentils

You're signed up for #cook90. Keep an eye on your inbox for the #cook90 starter guide.

~~Sugar lawtuc 1.99~~
~~Jam PC Strawberry~~ ~~.89~~ 1.16 $\frac{100}{mL}$
~~veg~~ Mango Ataulfo 1.49

~~4.99~~
~~2.89~~
~~1.49~~
~~6.37~~

Mango dessert
- cut in ~~half~~ or quarters
- put sugar on it
- cut red chilli pepper
- bake for 15 min at 350f
  keep eye on it.

Spicy chicken tortilla soup "
mix Presidents choice

1 small can tomatoe rose
1 lb ground beef
1 can Cambells small veg
        soup
mit from cambells

Bring to a boil
Simmer with lid for
about 25min.

— Fries   1 salt 3 pepper 6 evering
  2 potatoes (Shakes)   pie

— 5 burgers 1lb ground beef

— tomatoe onions romaine
  -1/2   1 whole   1 head

— 2 cups Brown rice   Boiling
      3 cups water   to mix
      1 can mushroom soup simmer
           (small)

— corn husks wrapped with mitten
      7 leave one corn

— Boil corn cut in half

— one carrot with a touch of
  sugar in water bullet or
  Juicer. 2 cups water 3

Spicy chicken tortilla soup
mix Presidents choice

1 small can tomatoe rose
1 lb ground beef
1 can Cambells small veg
    soup
mit from cambells

Bring to a boit
Simmer with lid for
about 25 min.

Search

eHow » Food & Drink » Appetizers, Soups & Salads » Condiments » How to Make Pico de Gallo

How to Make Pico de Gallo

By Christina Kalinowski
eHow Contributor

ⓟ   f   🐦   G+   ✉

26   7   Tweet   Share   Email   Save

A must at any fiesta, **pico de gallo** is an easy-to-make condiment consisting of finely diced onions, tomatoes and peppers that is welcome atop tacos and as a chip dip. More solid than soupy salsas, pico de gallo adds flavor and texture to any dish. Inspired by Serious Eats' Classic Pico de Gallo recipe, this version swaps out spicy chile peppers for green bell pepper and adds cumin to create a milder, earthier version.

Advertisement

Ingredients

- 1 medium-sized red onion, finely diced
- 4 ripe Roma tomatoes, finely diced
- 1/2 green bell pepper, finely diced
- 1 tablespoon fresh-squeezed lime juice
- 1 tablespoon fresh cilantro
- 1 teaspoon cumin
- Salt, to taste

Related Searches

Cheese Dip Recipe

Recipe for Making

Fresh Tomato Salsa Recipes

Chicken Recipe Recipes

Make Fresh Salsa

Handwritten notes:

July 2017 16 12:15 PM

took old el paso and fresh cilantro with salt.

drain tomatoes in strainer for 20–30 min add salt refrigerate in a freezer add pepper blend a jalapeño fresh cilanto

put in container for 3 days

paper towels, or put in a strainer. Let sit for 20 to 30 minutes to let the excess
moisture drain away from the tomatoes.

Step 2

Combine all of the ingredients in a bowl and mix well to combine. Taste and season
with additional salt, if necessary. Refrigerate for at least an hour before serving to
allow the flavors to meld.

Step 3

Store in a storage container in the refrigerator for up to 3 days.

Variations

If you like it hot, replace the green bell pepper with 1 to 2 finely diced **serrano or
jalapeno peppers**, or add a dash or two of **red pepper flakes**.

If you don't have fresh cilantro on hand, you can leave it out or substitute dried
cilantro, called coriander.

More of a technique than a hard-and-fast recipe, pico de gallo can accommodate
your personal taste and creativity. Add cubed fresh mango or pineapple, pomegranate
seeds, diced cucumber or jicama, cubes of avocado, chopped black olives or sliced
radish to vary your presentation.

Related Searches

You May Like

How to Make Shrimp
and Crab Ceviche -
No Raw Ingredients

How to Make Grilled
Fajitas

Greek Shrimp &
Mediterranean Salad
Recipes

How to Make Green
Tomato Chow Chow

Chicken Fajitas
Recipe

How to Freeze
Seafood Gumbo

Pre made CRUST for Apples Aug 8 2017 ①

Bake add sugar

1 pack of Cinamon — get

1 bunch Dill — get

6 clov garlic — get

3/4 Vinegar — get   Author ②
cup   2 sisters 2 citrus
6 table salt
6 spoons   mamma's
                       pickles

Cook time

2 day 9 minutes

cucumbers ends cut off

1. put garlic in botton of
mason jars, pickles sliced
into spears, some rings of dill
Lurst.

2 large bowl spout or measuring
cup mix together water, vinegar and salt
stir until salt is dissolved

place a few more sprigs of dill and
more pressed garlic on top
3. Refrigerate for 3 days.

- Salmon Ile Gran's recipe™
Salmon
Mashed potatoes margarine, milk
                    Salt pepper
Bake 375 - 20 min
      at 180℃.

- Soup
- chicken broth 1 can
  orange pepper
- red pepper
  Black beans (string)
- onion fried first
- carrot 2 [x] sticks whole
- One or almost almost whole tomatoe
- Salt pepper
- Dice veggies
- Boil 15 min then simmer
         2 top for 15 20 min

~~pepper~~ Black
- carrot
- tomatoe
- sauce from can (tomatoes)

Salad
— dress
  mayo, Apple cider, veg oil

— Black string beans (speared) (cut)
— rubarb?, like lettuce cut out
  Char?   stem
— tomatoe diced
— onion white diced
— red pepper diced
— orange pepper diced
— carrot 1 whole one diced
                cut in
                half Roast

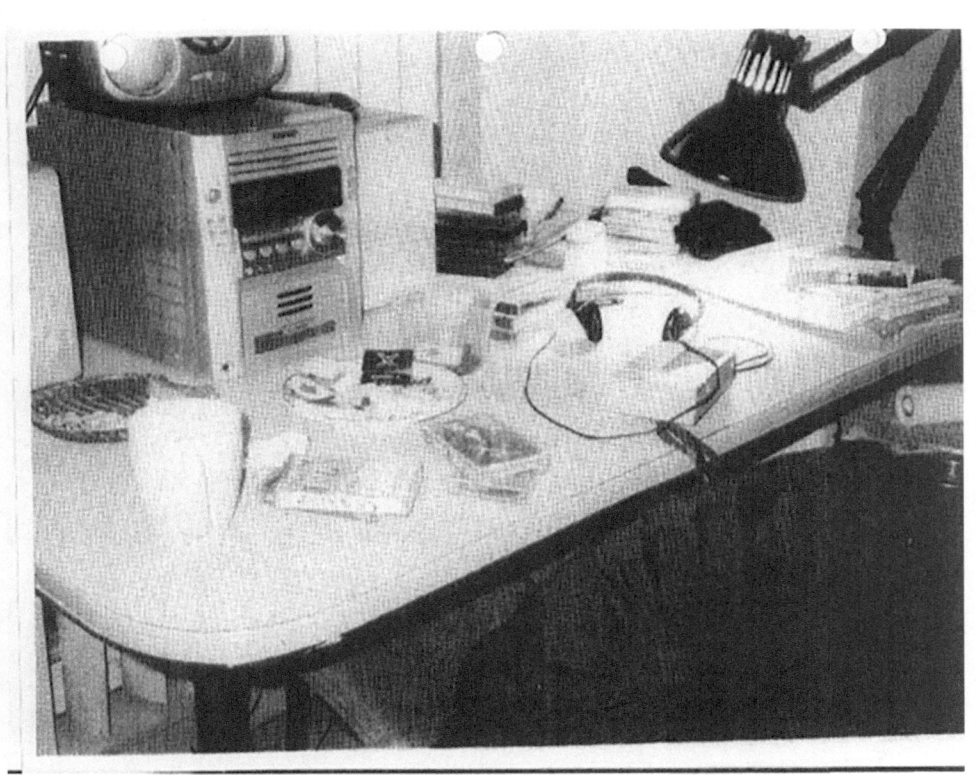

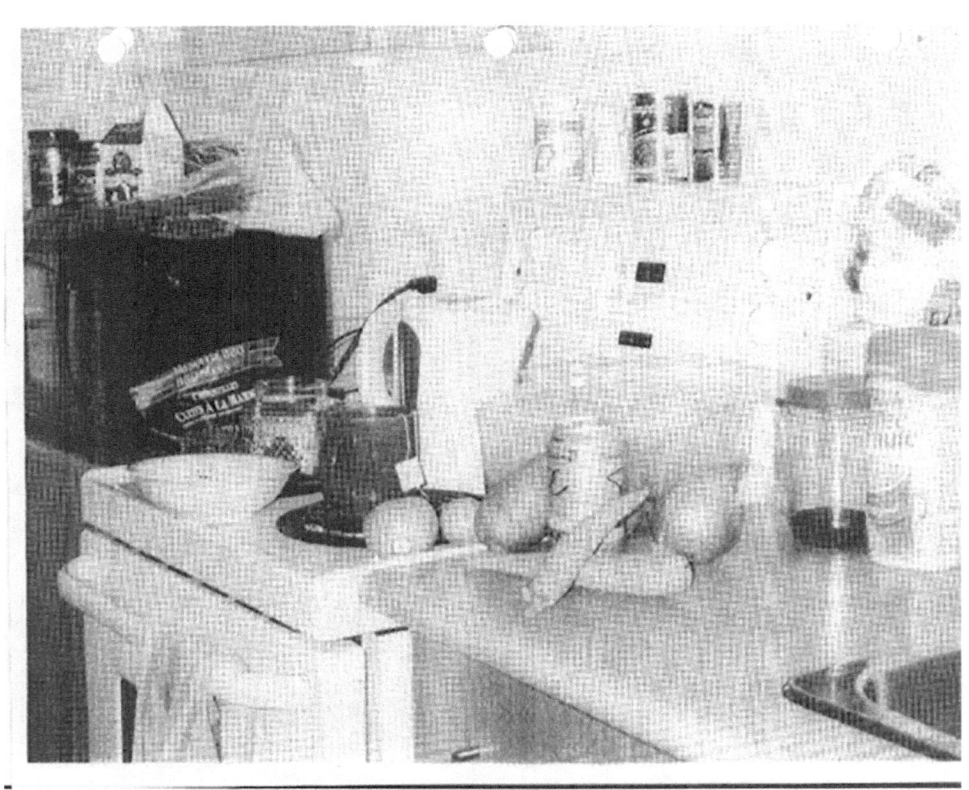

MATTHEW POPE

— ~~Campor-s chicken seimbo~~ — ~~out~~
small can
— Big crushed tomatoes
— cucumber (a lot)
— Beef root (cher)(Swiss cher).
small amount
— Cook potatoe one and half a
carrot first (diced) in frying
pan
— ~~one small amount of tomatoe~~
— crushed peppers spice

Salad
— Beet root
— cucumber
— tomatoe
— onion

Vingarette
white mayo
veg oil
Apple cider vinegar

casa aurelio

En la casa de comidas
más antigua del casco
histórico de Toledo.
¡Visita nuestra
corrala!

casa aurelio
calle sinagoga 6
reservas@casa-aurelio.com
925 22 20 97
687 858 282

33€ IVA INCL.

MENÚ ESPECIAL

PRIMER PLATO (A ELEGIR)

ENSALADA DE PIMIENTOS CONFITADOS CON
VENTRESCA, TOMATE PELADO Y MAJADO DE SIEMPRE
NUESTROS CALLOS CON GARBANZOS FINOS
SETAS CRUJIENTES CON FONDO DE SALMOREJO
MOLLEJAS DE CORDERO LECHAL SALTEADAS CON
SETAS, AJETES Y AZAFRÁN

SEGUNDO PLATO (A ELEGIR)

DEGUSTACIÓN DE ASADOS: CORDERO Y COCHINILLO
LOMO DE BACALAO CON ASADILLO DE LA HUERTA
DELICIAS DE CIERVO EN ESCABECHE TIBIO TOLEDANO

POSTRE (A ELEGIR)

SORBETE DE CREMA DE LIMÓN AL CAVA
CAÑITA RELLENA DE NATA NATURAL

incluye copa de vino, agua mineral, refresco o cerveza y café

www.casa-aurelio.com

---

casa aurelio

At the oldest eatery
in Toledo.
Visit our
inner court.

casa aurelio
calle sinagoga 6
925 22 20 97
687 858 282

33€ TAXES INCL.

SPECIAL MENU

FIRST COURSE (TO CHOOSE)

SUGAR COATED PEPPERS SALAD WITH TUNA FISH AND
PEELED TOMATO
OUR "CALLOS" (TRIPE BEEF MEAT) WITH FINE
CHICK PEAS
CRUNCHY MUSHROOMS WITH SALMOREJO (FRESH AND
TASTY TOMATO CREAM)
LAMB SWEETBREAD SAUTÉES WITH MUSHROOMS,
YOUNG GARLIC AND SAFFRON

SECOND COURSE (TO CHOOSE)

ROAST MEAT TASTING: LAMB AND PIGLET
COD SIRLOIN WITH A MIXTURE OF SLOW COOKED
VEGETABLES OF OUR GARDEN
DEER DELIGHTS COOKED WITH WARM MARINADE,
TYPICAL FROM TOLEDO

DESSERT (TO CHOOSE)

LEMON CREAM SHERBET WITH CAVA
PASTRY ROLLS FILLED WITH NATURAL CREAM

www.casa-aurelio.com

(/images/rcamedia/fotos_carta/sinagoga/carta-sinagoga-menu-especial-es.jpg) (/images/rcamedia/fotos_carta/sinagoga/carta-sinagoga-menu-especial-uk.jpg)

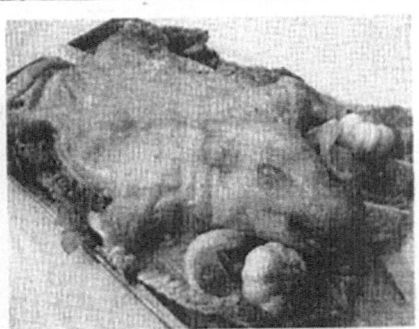

...ians

Iberian acorn ham	€ 21.80
Iberian loin of acorn	€ 21.80
Cheese from Manchego	€ 14.50
Assortment of Iberian	€ 23.00

Últimas noticias

Reservas (//reservas.html)

Casa Aurelio escenario del reality chino "Contigo-All over China" (//prensa/notas-de-prensa/item/63-np-20160219.html)

Ya ha llegado la Navidad a Casa Aurelio (//blog/item/62-ya-ha-llegado-la-navidad-a-casa-aurelio.html)

CASA AURELIO EN EL PROGRAMA CASTILLA-LA MANCHA EN EL CORAZON (25/07/2015) (//prensa/clipping/clipping-television/item/61-casa-aurelio-en-programa-castilla-la-mancha-en-el-corazon-rtvcm-25-7-2015.html)

CASA AURELIO EN EL PROGRAMA CASTILLA-LA MANCHA EN EL CORAZON (11/07/2015) (//prensa/clipping/clipping-television/item/60-casa-aurelio-en-programa-castilla-la-mancha-en-el-corazon-rtvcm-11-7-2015.html)

ABC, 10 de septiembre de 2015. (//prensa/clipping/clipping-prensa/item/59-abc-10-9-2015.html)

Lo más popular

Contacto

Oficina
C / Synogogue, 6
45001 Toledo
Spain
(tel:+34925224105) +34 925 224 105 (tel:+34925224105)

Synogogue
C / Synogogue, 6
45001 Toledo
(tel:+34925222097) +34 925 222 097 (tel:+34925222097)

town hall
Town Hall Square, 8
45001 Toledo
(tel:+34 925227716) +34 925 227 716 (tel:+34 925227716)

Mobile
(tel:+34687888282) +34 687 888 282 (tel:+34687888282)

Reservas@casa-aurelio.com (mailto:reservas@casa-aurelio.com)

About of

Just a stone's throw from La Catedral, El Alcázar or Las Sinagogas you will find Casa Aurelio Restaurants where you can enjoy in Toledo the best traditional cuisine accompanied by a wide variety of excellent wines from our winery.

(https://www.facebook.com/restaurantes.casaaurelio)

(https://twitter.com/Casa_Aurelio)

(http://es.linkedin.com/pub/casa-aurelio-restaurante/68/8/508)

(http://www.youtube.com/CasaAurelio)

Legal warning   Site Map   Credits
(/aviso-legal.html) (/site-map.html) (/creditos.html)

Block estroegen

Increase testoreone
meat

— Cook a week's meal in a
under hour.

phase 1   Block estrogen higher
          food blockers

phase 2 testoreone Boosting
        foods Recharge phase
phase 3   lean and toure body
          new base testoreone
          burning meals.

          Test mat nutrition

ROSS / Poetry   Sept 16 2007
            Drama teacher   (0)

log line / elevator pitch & Log line concept
one or two sentences long

concept
-refugees are sent to the past
to escape the future
(elevator pitch)
- travelling city devastation any Heartbreak

log line
who what when whey where
- Don't name person
Setting
a chef Hosto work with Coworker
to prevent a fight beren losing
the future goods.

a chef
a chef getting re aquainted with past
cook
members to Bring about another key
at neal pup to become or is a chef

a cook getting reacquainted with
former members to become an icon

pacific northwest in Seattle
5 min elevator pitch
COPS.
- Meal prep
- techniques
- Interpersonal skills
- give and take

absent minded meets masters
fish meeting the hook

Sophia Brown agency in California. YOUNG adult.
middle School.
COPS are good for concept
- High concept (Screen writing)
- more is elevator pitch
query letter in
synopsis summary on back of
Book!

* writer's digest Info.dawikaquinis.com
  successful query letters
    Chuck Sampathiwo

- Follow guidelines (send them what they ask for).
- Cut to the chase
- Staten why you pick the agent.
- query to a page
- Summary in Present tense
- no secrets
- Include word count
- mention experience
- Keep 1 2⁵ page synopsis.
- Treatments for Screen Play (15-20 pages)
  . cops instead
  - outline is a writer's tool like writing code for computers
  - write third person, conflicts, main characters
    resolution
    Nicole fellowship screenwriting

- Foreign Sales
- Audio Books

- Frankfurt Book Festival
- Do your own marketing
- go out and meet -
- small publishers queries
- Big house don't take queries

~~India Brown~~

Awp.com

Lamb chilli Oct 20
2017

- red pepper flakes
- chilli powder
- chopped garlic
- Red Kidney Beans
- Baked Beans
- onion
- lamb

Oct 51 COLT

eggplant
carrot
red pepper
green pickle like tomatoe
onion
potatoe

Diced and peeled
in oil and chopped garlic.
Bake at 400 F for 20min
then 200 until veggies
are tender every 12 min
TURN..

- wari gulf spinach
  kale + eggs
  luetin
  zeaxeanthins
  shellfish
      DHA
  xandu kakawdu plumfrut
      p
  Kangaroo meat.

  the outbreak
    vision protocol

3 potatoes
2 carrots
Black pepper
chopped garlic
Veggie oil

cut potatoes and carrots
into sticks
pre heat oven 425°
Bake 35-45 mins
let cool

Sauce

Kale

Onion (diced)

Carrot (2) (1C)

Mushroom Sauce
  P.Choice

1lb ground beef

BAFFLED BY BOMBER POWER HURRICANES SWITCH ATTACK

Poplowski Starts It, Don
Crowe Completes Charges
Originated by Stukus

Hayman Presents Revival "Three Men in a Hurry"

Crowe, Poplowski and Thompson Show
Stealers When Hurricanes Win Grey Cup

The Play That Decided Canadian Football Title

Dedicated to dear grandson Robin (our World Wide D.J.), our lovely Grand—daughter Cara and kind and clever John.

LANGUAGE AND THE MOTORIST

These are genuine extracts from motor claim forms received by a large insurance office in London, England.

1. The accident was due to the other man narrowly missing me.
2. Lorry halted and worked for the Corporation.
3. I collided with a stationary tramcar coming in the opposite direction.
4. The occupants were stalking dear on the hillside.
5. I left my Austin 7 outside, but when I cam out later, to my amazement, there was an Austin 12.
6. To avoid collision I ran into the other car.
7. There were plenty of lookers-on but no witnesses.
8. The water in my radiator accidentally froze at 12 midnight.
9. Car had to turn sharper than was necessary owing to an invisible lorry.
10. I was scraping my nearside on the bank when the accident happened.
11. After the accident a working gentleman offered to be a witness in my favour.
12. I collided with a stationary tree.
13. There was no damage done to the car as the gatepost will testify.
14. Accident was due to the road bending.
15. The witness gave his occupation as a gentleman, but it would be more correct to call him a garage proprietor.
16. The other man altered his mind and I had to run into him.
17. Ice on the road applied brakes causing skid.
18. I told the idiot what he was and went on.

19. One wheel went into the ditch. My foot jumped from brake to accelerator pedal, leapt across the road to the other side and jumped into the trunk of a tree.
20. I remember nothing after passing the Crown Hotel until I came to and saw P.C. Brown.
21. A cow wandered into my car, I was afterwards informed that the cow was half-witted.
22. A bull was standing near and a fly must have tickled him because he gored my car.
23. She suddenly saw me, lost her head and we met.
24. I was taking a friend home and keeping two yards from each lamp post which were in a straight line. Unfortunately there was a bend in the road bringing the right hand lamp post in line with the other and of course I landed in a ditch.
25. If the other driver had stopped a few yards behind himself, it would not have happened.
26. I bumped into a shop window and sustained injuries to my wife.
27. I bumped into the lamp post which was obscured by human beings.
28. I heard a horn blow and was struck violently in the back. Evidently a lady was trying to pass me.
29. I misjudged a lady crossing the street.
30. Coming home I drove into the wrong house and collided with a tree I haven't got.
31. Three women were talking to each other, and when two stepped back and one stepped forward I had to have an accident.
32. I can't give details of the accident as I was somewhat concussed at the time.
33. Willful damage to the upholstery was done by rats.
34. A pedestrian hit and went underneath my car.
35. I blew my horn but it would not work as it was stolen.
36. A lamp post bumped into my car, damaging it in two places.
37. My car was stolen and I set up a human cry, but it has not been recovered.

38. The car in front stopped suddenly and I crashed gently into his luggage grid.
39. I left my car unattended for a minute, and whether by accident or design it ran away.
40. The other car collided with me, without giving warning of his intention.
41. I unfortunately ran over a pedestrian and the old gentlemen was taken to hospital, much regretting the circumstances.
42. On entering Wales I blew my horn at the left hand corner.
43. I thought the side window was down but it was up as I found out when I put my head through it.
44. I considered neither vehicle was to blame, but if either was to blame it was the other one.
45. I was proceeding along the road at moderate speed when another car rushed out of a side turning and turned upside down in a ditch. It was his fault as he said.
46. I knocked over a man, he admitted it was his fault as he had been knocked down before.
47. I looked for the sign but the more I looked the more I couldn't find it.

ACHTUNG!

ALLES TOURISTEN UND NON-TECHNISCHEN LOOKENS PEEPERS! DAS MACHINE KONTROL IS NICHT FÜR GERFINGERPOKEN UND MITTENGRABBEN. ODERWISE IS EASY SCHNAPPEN DER SPRINGENWERK, BLOWENFUSE, UND POPPENKORKEN MIT SPITZENSPARKEN. DER MACHINE IS DIGGEN BY EXPERTEN ONLY, IS NICHT FÜR GERVERKEN BY DAS DUMMKOPFEN. DAS RUBBERNECKEN SIGHTSEENEN KEEPEN DAS COTTON PICKEN HANDS IN DAS POCKETS SO RELAXEN UND BEN WATCHEN DAS BLINKENLIGHTS.

Compliments of GARET TOOL COMPANY L

THANKS AND FAREWELL

Thank you very much, Dear Reader, for seeing this thro' to the end with me. I would like to finish in a note of Thankfulness, for my wonderful life, the blessings of good health and the love and loyalty of my beloved family and friends:

This little poem's just for you.
My Friends and Family—
To thank you for the love and help
You've always shown to me.
We've had our Joy,
We've had our Bumps,
We've had our In-Betweens—,

But—Boy-oh-Boy-

You've Turned up Trumps—

The Best of "Human Beans"!
—x—

I would dearly love to mention you all by name, but am afraid of unintentionally missing someone out, so I will just say, with love, "**You** know who you are!" See you in Book 2. Bless you all!
—x—

Things I have learned:

When folks cry in anguish about "Life", "What does it **TAKE…?!**"— from my own humble experience, an honest answer would be

It takes:

All of your Strength, Humour, Patience, Kindness, Tenacity and Faith— but above all—LOVE (which sounds gentle, easy and comfy-cozy, but is actually the toughest bit of all.)

Just a thought for those less fortunate of the world:

I saw the following "Oxfam" notice on the wall of a London Tube Station recently:

"Everyone's entitled to a few of life's Luxuries—food, water, and little things like that…"

So—may you yourself be blessed, "FARE WELL" and "Go on your way Rejoicing" (See p.19) Hope to see you in Book 2! (So glad I finally got it all together, even if I have forgotten where I put it… What was my name again…?)

APPENDIX

I n spite of many sad events (that happen to us all) I have had a very well- blessed life, and have been given the strength to endure and also even enjoy it! Some of the high points being:

1. Going UP in a Hot Air Balloon
2. Going DOWN a Coalmine in Wales. (Hubby dug out our very own lump of coal!)
3. A couple of Flying Lessons (Decided the cost of continuing, tho' fair, would be too high for me)
4. Visits to: The Grand Canyon, Yellowstone Park, Disneyland (L.A.), Hollywood, New York, San Francisco, Chicago, Miami, Montana, Minnesota, Seattle, Hawaii, Mexico, Spain, The Rockies (Canada), Toronto, Calgary, Vancouver (& Island), Banff Newfoundland (since being born there), Germany, Majorca, Tenerife, Amste.
5. Living in: Abbots Langley (Herts) circa 1136,
    Torquay and Paignton (Devon) Milton Keynes (Bucks.) circa 1970 Germany (Dusseldorf and Hmaburg)
    London England: Wembley and Cricklewood Edgware (middlesex), England
    Calgary, Vancouver (Canada) (in log cabins)
6. The best of all: my secure and happy upbringing
    My family and friends
    My happy marriage and the birth of our two fine children and the joy of my grandchildren
7. My Bonus Point: I'M STILL HERE!
    What's more lucky enough to have Residency Rights for two of the world's best (and still gentlest) countries— dear ole U.K. and beautiful Canada.

My grandfather John Pope was a good man, he always took care of the kids and had options on how to help us.

He made 800 dollars a month during his time with the CFL. He supported me in my business adventures. He did live long enough to see me have some success. My grandmother Maddy John's wife was also very nurturing. She had lots of meals for us when we came to visit. My grandfather Horace Ernst East, who I never met was also quite the person I Hear from my dad Greg. My grandmother on his side lived to 103 and she was a farm girl. My grandfather Paddy was also neat, he bought me brown leather shoes which lasted awhile, I even walked 22km in them to raise money for a charity in Ok Falls. My grandmother Lorraine was always saying to ask questions.

My grandfather I never met from my maternal grandmother's side as he passed away from working on the airplanes in world war 2 from leukemia. She wrote the book included in this novel. My grandmother Louise supported us in the trades of work. I worked for the family's construction company and Sel would always pick me up. Made too much money back then.